ILLUSTRATED BY ISAAC BRAMBLE
GARY BLACKFORD

WINNING
BETWEEN THE
EARS

CREATING PATHWAYS TO TRANSFORMATION

Ark House Press
PO Box 1722, Port Orchard, WA 98366 USA
PO Box 1321, Mona Vale NSW 1660 Australia
PO Box 318 334, West Harbour, Auckland 0661 New Zealand
arkhousepress.com

© 2017 Gary Blackford

All rights reserved. No part of this publication may be reproduced, stored in a retrieval system or transmitted in any form or by any means electronic, mechanical, photocopying, recording or otherwise without the prior written permission of the publisher.

Gary Blackford
gary@garyblackford.com
www.garyblackford.com

Cataloguing in Publication Data:
Title: Winning Between the Ears
ISBN: 978-0-6481734-2-7 (pbk.)
Subjects: Christian Living,
Other Authors/Contributors: Blackford, Gary

Cover image and illustrator: Isaac Bramble
Design and layout by initiateagency.com

CONTENTS

Darth Vader	1
Machete Mayhem	6
Scared half to death	12
So Weird	13
Rattling cages	15
Extremist	17
Mind the Meds	22
Making Headway	26
Out of control	28
Choice	32
Biblical Neuroscience	36
Busy Brain	39
Pepperoni	44
Up frontal	48
Riding a Hippo	50
Accessorising	53
Bubble	61
North	69
Napoleon	71
Cool Runnin's Man	76
Wide	86
Will	89
Now	92
Reruns	95
Destructive memory loops	97
Focal-ism	99
Tardis	101
So far so good	108
Breakfast	110
Motivate	116
Total transformation	122
About the author	124

DARTH VADER

He grew up in a middle class suburban family. Mum and dad with four children. A nice family home with parents who although not perfect, sacrificed in order to give their children the best start to life. Working hard, his father made ends meet, and to look at the household, you'd see it how it truly was; a good family, growing and living in middle class suburban Sydney, Australia. Free from war or the fear of war, childhood was filled with cricket games in the backyard while destroying his mother's flower gardens, football matches, wrestling with his brothers, building and playing with model aeroplanes, fire cracker nights and more cricket. Yet sickness was his constant companion. His system filled with steroids, this chronic asthmatic body struggled to breathe. His parents would lay awake for hour upon hour at night listening to him struggle for breath. Each night was filled with the possibilities of late night emergency wards, breathing clinics and medication. A lover of sport, he dreamed of representing his country in almost every sport, yet ever-present physical challenges crushed all hope. Many days absent due to sickness, set him behind and struggling with school. With both elder siblings progressing well in their education, the pressure was on to achieve. Yet for some unknown reason, he could not understand simple words, sentence structure or maths, and comprehension and retention of information seemed to be elusive. Not till he had struggled within the school system for years did he discover, through illness while watching daytime television, that this new discovery they were discussing was how he'd existed for years. Listening intently to doctors discussing how for some people, words move on the page and how although the sufferer of Dyslexia can have perfect sight, the wiring of the brain struggles to focus, understand, comprehend and retain information. In an instant he knew they were describing him. On that fateful day in the lounge room of that middle-class family home, he took another step down a dangerous pathway. For this adolescent, not only was he the worthless sick kid, this day he became the stupid kid whose brain was not 'normal.' This compounded his already developing self-disapproval. What he had developed were neural networks that ran past his core belief that he was useless and worthless (because to him all the evidence proved it).

It seemed that everything in life would compound and place layer upon layer of memories that all revolved around and re-enforced his inability to be what he perceived as 'normal.' Failing school, ridiculed for breathing like 'Darth Vader', he turned to relationships, and although some were good, so much self-loathing only meant that co-dependence would result and his heart broken on several occasions.

Always having a deep desire to serve his country, he left school as early as possible, attempting to join the military. Failing the medical, despite drugging himself on so much asthma medication that his hands shook for days, another failure turned him toward alcohol. At least with alcohol he could stop his mind, for by now his mind perpetually raced and would not slow down. Haunted by a recurring nightmare, fear consumed the days and dread dominated the nights.

DARTH VADER

Anxiety would now rack his body and fear grew seemingly daily. What was it that wanted him gone? Nights would be filled with fitful terror, voices from within told him he was lost, worthless, a mistake and he could never achieve or amount to anything worthwhile. Although he was determined to make his life count and went about putting the trapping of success around him so that everybody would see that he was okay, he wasn't okay. Debt increased to perpetuate a false image, while sliding ever fast down a slope towards disaster. His thought life, now out of control, dominated every hour. Self-harm, self-hate and increasing terror was the only existence he knew. Destroying relationships with family and friends, getting further into debt, smashing cars, taking crazy risks, and all the time knowing he was approaching the end game - suicide.

Surviving an attempt at suicide, he received a sniff of hope that quickly dissipated in fear. Till one day after smashing his car, sitting in a loan vehicle outside that same family home, broken, confused and traumatised his mind and body finally collapsed. It had run so fast for so long. It had driven him to wild hallucinations and hellish visions. The tension and trauma compounded with fear induced sleep deprivation, till this perfect storm of self-loathing, shattered dreams and a broken mind simply stopped, it shut down. So there he sat, broken, slumped over the wheel, not moving, barely breathing. For how long, who knows? Exhaustion, utter fatigue overwhelmed him.

From this point on others would attempt to fix him. There was a blur of hospitals, examinations, doctors, specialists and family members wondering what had happened.

I have been working closely with this young man for a long time. We have battled together through many dank, dark, cold, wet, bleak, barren, difficult days, and enjoyed the bright, beautiful, basking-in-the-sun drenched mountain top days as well. This journey has been filled with ups, downs, valleys and mountain tops and what is amazing is that if you met this guy now, you'd never even consider where he'd come from. Unless he told you his story, for which this is only a brief excerpt, you'd never know. Why?

It's because his brain circuitry has been changed. His mind has been altered and in truth renewed to the point that, although he remembers what he suffered, it's like he's remembering a different person. This has not been achieved through some experimental operation performed by an elite surgical team. In essence, this book is all about how this has happened, and although each and everyone's personal story is different, and every life has various obstacles and challenges, this miraculous tale of transformation that draws its deliverance as much from ancient texts as modern neuroscience, is one that hopefully will inspire you to your core. Enjoy!

The once dominating, destructive, neural pathways and loathsome, layered memories have been replaced with better pathways and loving layered memories. His core beliefs of self-hate and his identity based in failure, sickness and pain, have now been re-written. He is now a new man. Where once anxiety dominated every waking hour, peace and security rule. Where fear once paralysed his life almost stealing away his existence, now trust, hope and love fill his life with joy beyond imagining.

I hope no one reading these pages can fully identify with this man. I hope you cannot completely connect and that your life has not been consumed by utter hopelessness. I do however hope that you grasp the principles that have revolutionised this man's life. I am passionate about teaching everyone what you'll discover in these pages. Although these pages don't contain every answer to life, they certainly contain many.

A new path to the river awaits. A new re-wired and transformed mind awaits those who are searching. Our thinking processes result in neurological pathways being created within our mind. These pathways are strengthened as they are used. Therefore, the longer we think a certain way, the stronger that way or thinking becomes. To change the way we think we must create new neurological networks within our mind and set about strengthening them through repetition. The miracle of mind renewal happens when these new thought processes become habitual. The dominant habit will always win; therefore repetition changes the dominance of one thought process, replacing it with another. It's when these habits are created the mind is re-wired, thus totally altering our destiny.

How do I know this? How can I assure you with such clarity of purpose?

How can I, an author you may have never met, know your mind or the individual traumas that have shaped you? While it's true that I don't know your individual circumstances, I can assure you that the principles laid out within these pages will help you. Why?

Because I am the man you were just introduced to.

If you guessed it, well done!

I know, I really know how it is to be broken and desperately lost. I know the difficulty and determination it takes to create the habits that re-write the mind. This has been nothing short of a knockdown, drag out, fight to the death. Thankfully the death of destructive thinking and the emergence of life giving thoughts have established a brand new being.

Wherever you are on life's journey, a better brain awaits!

So get your machete out, we're about to start cutting through to your best future.

Are you ready?

MACHETE MAYHEM

A new path to the river

Imagine with me for a moment you're in a forest. You live in this forest, and have for some time. Your home is a delightful log cabin amidst the tall trees. Part of your daily routine is fetching water from the crystal-clear glacier-fed stream that flows about half a mile away. The first few times you went to the stream there was no defined path. You tried a few ways and settled on one route. Then every day you've taken the same path. That rough track through the forest has become more defined, the twigs that crossed the path are pushed aside, the grass has given way to forest floor and it's much easier to walk that path now. You've walked it so often, you don't even think about it anymore. There's even a small indentation or rut developing on the path. So routine is this trip that you simply do what you did yesterday, and the day before.

Our thinking processes function in much the same way. Once we establish neural pathways our thinking moves down these pathways much like water always flows to the point of least resistance. The brain is designed to quickly identify shortcuts and use the most efficient and well-defined routes. Like your path to the river your neural pathways are strengthened each time we travel them. The synapses (or joining points within our thought processes) form stronger bonds through usage. To win between the ears in the context of our illustration is to choose to take a new path to the river. What I'm asking you to do is to firstly and consciously stop taking the established pathways and repeatedly choose to take a better way to the river. If you're happy to always do what you've always done, nothing will change. Albert Einstein stated, "Insanity: doing the same thing over and over again and expecting different results."[1] If you want things to always be as they have been, then what are you doing reading this book anyway? However, your 'best you' will be found in the new path to the river. Deciding to take a new path to the river is to decide on a better way, a way full of transformed thinking for our lives.

Let's consider this as we begin - this new path, how will it greet you? Will the forest of low branches, undergrowth, long grasses, fallen trees and other forest debris suddenly, with just one choice, prayer or spontaneous thought, miraculously pull back and create a beautiful clear unhindered pathway? Will the trees become an archway and the forest grasses transform to a marble lane ushering you effortlessly towards the life-giving stream where you can dance and skip along filled with sweet tranquility? How I wish that were true. The opposite awaits you my friend. This is not a journey for the faint hearted. The new path will be rough at first, more like hacking through dense bush undergrowth with a machete. You've not walked this way before, or maybe not for a long time. There will be obstacles that need to be removed and webs to entangle you. You'll be stepping over logs, broken branches and your feet will be saturated from the grass that still covers the way. Let's face facts, to take a new path to the river will be hard at first. In fact, the old path will be tempting.

---

1 Einstein, Albert. BrainyQuote.com http://www.brainyquote.com/quotes/quotes/a/alberteins133991.html (Accessed 29th November 2016)

Your mind will want to go the old way, as it is already established, clear and less hassle. Some days you'll even step from your cabin before the caffeine has kicked in and simply, on autopilot, head down the old pathway. Our shortcut driven minds will automatically head the established way, even if that way is not the best for us. Yet you know there is a new path that needs to be established, a new way of thinking that's actually a better way, therefore each day you make a choice. This choice is a conscious decision that takes place in the decision making centre of our brain within our frontal lobe. We make this conscious choice day after day to take the new better path. Guess what happens? Although the old path still remains (just like our old neural networks remain), the new one, over time, becomes better defined and easier. After a while it takes a lot less thought, and you simply take the better way to the river. It has been said that it takes about thirty days to create a good habit. Sadly, from my experience, it takes only about thirty seconds to create a bad one. That aside, when a new way of thinking is consciously and constantly chosen the end result is new neurological pathways. This process will take about a month of purposeful choices, to begin to create and establish new mind pathways that function habitually. This is literally a renewing of the mind process. This re-wiring of our thinking is available to everyone breathing. It involves taking captive thoughts and choosing which to accept or reject. It's actually the self-discipline of choosing the new way to the river that brings about the transformed mind we all desire.

I don't think there would be a person on earth who would not agree that the greatest battles we ever face are between our ears.

The greatest battles we ever face are between our ears.

Each of us has a unique journey. All of us have come through various challenges and we all have well-established neural pathways. Some of these pathways may have been birthed in trauma or established in insecurity, or through positive reinforcement of a parent or loved one.

Let's consider our thinking for a moment. It's amazing how little we generally think about our thinking. How would your life change for the better, if by the end of this book, you were set free from any distracting or destructive thought patterns? What if within these pages you find, or at least take significant steps toward discovering your unique self? Even as you learn how to control, direct and re-orientate your thought life, you will be changed. To win between our ears is to win in life. So come with me, embark on a new way to the river today. I can lead you there, only because as you'll discover, my mind was broken and almost beyond repair. I love my mind, now. This mind of mine, which has opened up life in all its beauty, is the same mind that once haunted my every hour with paralyzing fear and utter despair. Although I say it's my same mind, it is actually not. I have not had a brain transplant, so technically it's the same brain, but it has been re-wired and therefore is a different mind. It's still the engine that drives me, yet it's an engine that's been overhauled and rebuilt, and the difference is astounding. I know what it takes to renew a mind, and let me say from the outset, it is a battle and you will not win every fight. This is not however the goal; the goal is to win the war. Make no mistake, a war it is. The undergrowth will be thick and the way difficult. This will be a disciplined pursuit. It's an aggressive revolutionary mindset of letting nothing hinder you. Why? Because when you start, everything will try to stop you. The mind once set, is proven to resist change. However, correct understanding of what we're doing physically, spiritually and scientifically will show us the way, and deliver confidence in the process. However, it's intentional that we bring our willpower, determination and stubborn pig-headed persistence to the equation. Our willpower will be fundamental in birthing the routines that become habits that transform our lives. It will not be easy nor instant. You're about to embark on a journey and this journey of discovery, like any great adventure, will be filled with mighty oceans to cross, mountains to climb and deep dark valleys to be traversed. Is it worth it? Oh Yeah!

The greatest battles we ever face are between our ears.
The flow of our lives is directed from our minds and therefore a mind transformed changes everything. It's said that the great polar explorer Earnest Shackleton, when preparing to depart England for the Antarctic, placed an advertisement 'Men Wanted: For hazardous journey, small wages, bitter cold, long months of complete darkness, constant danger, safe return doubtful, honour and recognition in case of success.'[2] Their subsequent journey has become legend and their pioneering spirit has inspired many. This book is not for those who would shy back from an adventure. Although one does not need to consider oneself brave, brave you must be. It's for those who realise that we have but one life to live, who understand that what we do in this life matters, and that how we think changes everything. So no matter the metaphor you prefer, you can see yourself standing on the deck of the Endurance sailing with Shackleton for the icy Antarctic, or grabbing a machete, stepping out of your log cabin and beginning to slash at the thick undergrowth. What matters most right now is the answer to this simple question - In this journey that will take you

---

2 Cool Antarctica. Shackleton Endurance Expedition-Trans-Antarctica 1914-1917-page.1. http://www.coolantarctica.com/Antarctica%20fact%20file/History/Shackleton-Endurance-Trans-Antarctic_expedition.php (Accessed 28th November 2016)

to the very limits of yourself, that will challenge and touch the core of your being, yet become the journey that will define, redefine and transform your life in more ways than imaginable, are you up for it?

"Never for me the lowered banner, never the last endeavour."
Sir Ernest Shackleton[3]

---

[3] Jarvis, Tim. *Shackleton's Epic: Recreating the world's greatest journey of survival.* Harper Collins Publishers. Sydney Australia.

SCARED HALF TO DEATH

'Oh, I hope this goes well, its new material. Now in front of the largest audience I've ever spoken to before, I'm going to present as yet 'un-road tested' material.' These were the thoughts that ran through my mind and played on my nerves. I knew the science added up, the connections were true and I knew I needed to try. I had a sense that something very special was about to take place, but what, I did not know. I hoped to articulate well, as I knew this profound mind renewal process could change many lives. I just knew that if this group of precious people grabbed and implemented these principles, then their lives would be transformed just like mine had been. The response was stunning with almost everyone in the packed auditorium acknowledging how these principles would help them battle and overcome their thoughts. That 35 minute talk has touched countless lives since, and has become the essence of these pages before you. It became, in the words of many that day, a 'game changer.' A game changer for the listeners and a game changer for me as I saw the need and response to what I'm about to share with you.

SO WEIRD

Standing on the streets of Chennai, India, my heart broke as I watched a child of maybe 10 to 12 years old, drag herself behind a group of westerners begging. As a father of four daughters, this young Indian girl with legs crippled, moving by hand-power, was a reality check. You don't have to be there long to realise just how blessed the majority of us truly are. It's one of those weird things, that when people see me standing before crowds or watch me with my family and all the joy I have in being me, that it's at times simple to think that life has been good and relatively easy. It's true, I have a great life. I profess to many that I am the most blessed man alive. As an author, speaker, father and husband I am blessed. I have a life the vast majority of the world would envy. Yet it has not always been that way. I write these pages from a place of genuine happiness and strength mentally, emotionally and physically (although the physical always needs work), yet not for a moment do I forget where I've come from. Although I did not grow up in the slums of India, my mind has been as broken and as useless as that young lady's legs.

Unique

We are body, soul, mind and spirit. We are mental, emotional, spiritual, intellectual beings. Therefore the approach within these pages is holistic. It makes no sense to become successful outwardly while falling apart inwardly. So in order to positively affect our entire being, we must approach the subject of 'Winning between the Ears' from multiple angles. The goal is to win in life. This does not mean to be better than anyone else or to win over others, it simply means for each individual to be their unique self and fulfill their divine mission on planet earth. I believe that each of us are precious individuals with a purpose to fulfill during our time here. I also believe that each of us has a unique self, a place where we are at our purest and most fulfilled. A place where our unique self, in whatever forms that takes, discovers and lives in all the fullness of why we're on this blue dot in space. This unique self is different for everyone; therefore it's unique to you. What we can accomplish when living in our unique self is mind-boggling. It may be to rescue children from the horrors of human trafficking in Nepal, to raise children to be confident adults, to sow your gift in business to fund missions around the world. Whatever it is, I think we're not only the happiest, but we're the most fulfilled in the zone of fulfilling our unique purpose.

RATTLING CAGES

One of the most impactful and naturally sad sights I've ever seen was in one of the strangest places. Some of our family members were pastoring a church in a little country town called Guyra, in New South Wales. New South Wales is an eastern state of Australia and Guyra, population of around 2000 people, is a small high-altitude town. Once while visiting in Guyra, we jumped in our cars and headed about 45minutes west to a place called Green Valley Farm. Green Valley Farm is a rural self-styled, family constructed, 'sort of' theme park. When I say theme park, if images of Disneyland, Sea World or Dreamworld come to mind, it is certainly not these! It's not close to any major population area. With rides made of metal and springs, a strange museum, and a very different type of petting zoo, Green Valley Farm is an eclectic, leaning toward eccentric, wonderland. Smiths' museum is there, boasting all sorts of things in jars. 'Come see the two- headed calf or an eight-legged chicken' is an advertising slogan. Who would put the world's largest recorded Kangaroo testicles in a jar? Why measure them? Who measures them? Does that give you an idea of this place? It's all on line, (not the Kangaroo testicles)!

Check it out and if you ever get a chance, visit. We had a great time with the children. There's a petting zoo, where (I kid you not) you can pat a five-legged sheep and six-legged cow. (Personally, I was thinking there must be a nuclear waste dump nearby). There are also deer, kangaroos, a wombat, monkeys and more. While there, I walked over a small rise. A sight came into view that still, many years later, is vivid, branded in my mind's eye. There before us was a massive eagle. The biggest I'd ever seen. Eagles are majestic creatures, equipped to ride the thermals and soar to great heights. They are powerful yet stunningly beautiful. What struck me as so sad about this eagle was that it was in a cage. I cannot tell you why it was there and possibly for a perfectly good reason, but the image of this beautiful bird stuck and restricted in a cage has never left me. This image reminds me of so many people I meet, as I travel and speak, concerning the mind and its renewal. Precious people, so paralysed by their past that they miss the miracle of the moment, and in many cases forgo their future, because they're trapped in a cage and cannot seem to get out.

So, I'm on a mission, to unlock some cages. Your mission, (if you choose to accept it) is to fly free as an eagle. Before you get too excited, there is however a warning attached to this mission. In order to unlock some cages, I may have to rattle a few cages in the process. So as we progress, if you think I'm rattling your cage a little, or a lot, can you trust me? I'm just trying to free the latch so you can come out and begin to spread your wings again, or for the first time launch from the perch of the past and start to soar into all your future may hold.

EXTREMIST

After his initial disappointment as being described as an extremist, Dr. Martin Luther King Jr. stated, "I gradually gained a bit of satisfaction from being considered as extremist... Was not Abraham Lincoln an extremist: "This nation cannot survive half slave and half free." Was not Thomas Jefferson an extremist: "We hold these truths to be self-evident, that all men are created equal." So the question is not whether we will be extremists but what kind of extremists will we be." [4] I must confess to you today, I am an extremist. I believe everybody, no matter their station in life, no matter the state of their emotions or the complexity of issues around their mental wellbeing, can be positively influenced and helped through these pages.

I have an extreme view of humanity; I believe that everyone is of value. I believe that every soul is precious and that none should be left behind or alone. I know my philosophy flies in the face of modern secularism that promotes the absence of personal value. My extreme view is that while there is breath in our lungs, there is hope for the future. I know that some sectors of the scientific community promote humanity as nothing more than the result of a random sequence of code that somehow crawled from a primeval swamp to become man-

---

4 King, Martin Luther Jr. *Dream. The words and inspiration on Martin Luther King Jr.* Hachette Australia Level 17, 207 Kent St Sydney NSW 2000Australia Dream p.52

kind. I profoundly disagree. I believe that while humanity and society may evolve in many respects, the building blocks of life have the divine all over them. Charles Darwin in the famed 'The Origin of Species' states, "To suppose that the eye with all its inimitable contrivances for adjusting the focus to different distances, for admitting different amounts of light, and for the correction of spherical and chromatic aberration, could have been formed by natural selection, seems, I freely confess, absurd in the highest degree."[5] He is right. The formation and complexity of a seeing eye is beyond the realm of chance and squarely in the miraculous.

Love a Smoothie
'Holistic health' is our mission while learning to win between our ears. Because life flows from the thoughts, if we get the thinking right, we in turn get life right.

Using modern scientific discoveries, ancient biblical texts and personal experience while adding in a slice or two of fun, we'll blend them all together and create a smoothie for life. It's not the famed elixir of life that promises eternal youth, alas we will all age. Sorry to break that to you. Yet as we blend these parts together we see that they all come together harmoniously. This human brain between our ears is the most amazing piece of technology on the planet. As we explore the mind, science and spirituality we shall see the pieces of the puzzle of life coming together perfectly. Dr. Timothy Jennings uses a term 'Harmonized Truth.'[6] This is the central area where science, experience and scripture cross over. The danger comes when we take any of these particular areas and view them as the

---

5 Darwin, Charles. *The Origin of Species*, J.M. Dent & Sons Ltd, London 1971, p.167

6 Jennings, Timothy R. *The God-Shaped Brain 'How changing your view of God transforms your life.'* InterVarsity Press. Downers Grove, IL 60515-1426

EXTREMIST

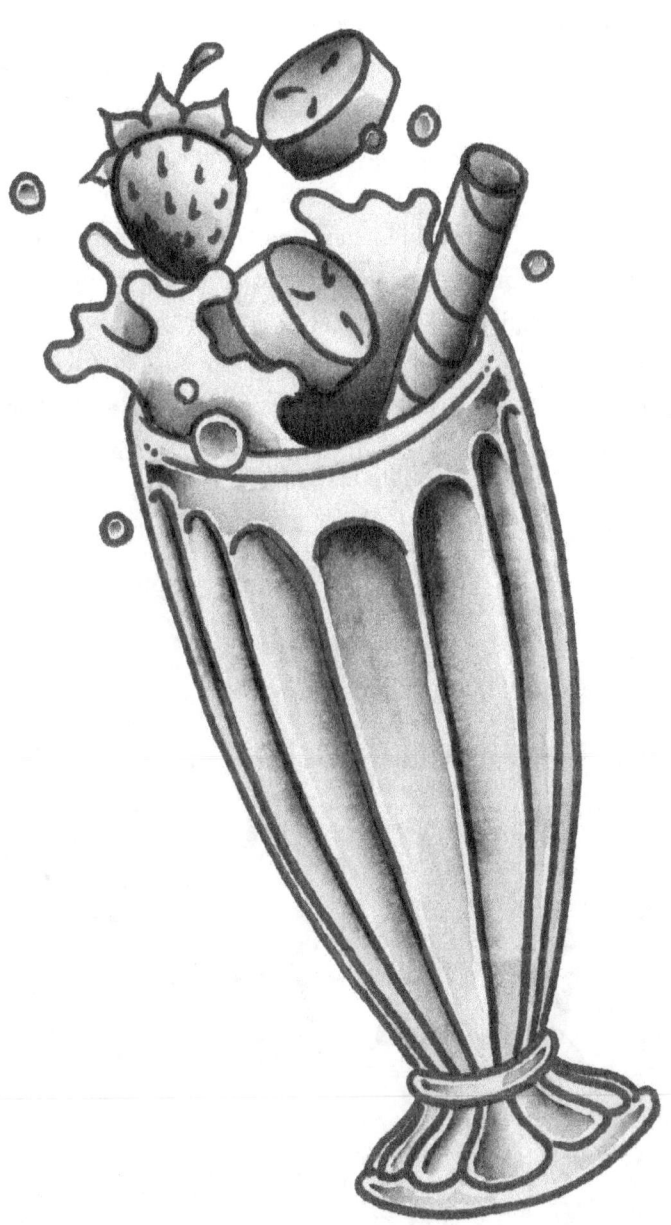

whole picture. Focusing on one piece of the puzzle and proclaiming it as a whole will inevitably and invariably result in error. For instance, if I was to view everything related to the mind as a scientific or chemical related problem, then the end result is to add or subtract chemicals and that should fix everything. Therefore we add more and more drugs to fix psychological problems. This has led to a chemically overprescribed society that only masks problems that need holistic remedies - therefore just throwing more and more chemicals at a suffering individual has led to error. Although they are pieces in the puzzle, they're not the whole picture. If I were to view everything as spiritual, error would be the result as well. The great biblical teacher Dr. Martin Lloyd Jones states; "Many...in fact, are in

utter ignorance concerning this realm where the borderlines between the physical, psychological and spiritual meet. Frequently I have found that such leaders had treated those whose trouble was obviously mainly physical or psychological, in a purely spiritual manner and if you do so, you not only don't help you aggravate the problem."[7]

We are spiritual beings as well as physical. The reality is people can suffer from depression simply because of the foods they consume. Therefore running around trying to make out there is some demonic spirit in the room and casting it out is ludicrous. If it's not spiritual, why make it that way? The spiritual aspect is important and a necessary piece in the jigsaw but regarding everything as a spiritual problem will inevitably lead to error.

Experience can also lead to error simply because we all experience life differently. I could overcome something in my life by making one key decision, yet for another who perhaps has suffered significant trauma around the same area, it could take years to overcome. Therefore a harmonised approach is vital.

---

[7] Jones, Martyn Lloyd *The Christian Warfare* (Grand Rapids: Baker, 1976), 206-208.

MIND THE MEDS

A moment's meditation regarding medication
In a western world where current figures suggest that conservatively speaking one in every four people are suffering from mental or emotional challenges, depression and anxiety levels have risen sharply and the proliferation of medication now sees vast numbers of people taking various types of mood stabilizing treatments. This compels me to take a few moments to discuss medication. I come across many people who take a mood stabilising medication under a medical professional's supervision while traversing challenges of life. The crazy thing is that because I speak in many church/spiritual environments, I find so many people live in guilt because they take the medication. I find this quite disturbing, as in my view these (church) environments should be the most positive and uplifting places on earth. I would go as far as saying, that I believe a healthy local church (which is people, not a building or denomination), is the best environment on earth for someone struggling mentally or emotionally to recover fully. That is however under the proviso that we get the process of recovery and renewal right. If not, the risk is high for alienation, disillusionment and destruction of hope. No one will ever reach their unique self and full potential through guilt, hence these few moments around the subject

of medication. Even if you're not on medication yourself, without doubt you'll know someone who is. We know that a very large proportion of people who eventually see a doctor, specialist, or some sort of mental health professional will, in our current environment, be placed on mood-stabilising medication. In some cases this medical treatment may be entirely necessary and can literally save lives.

Without doubt, the greatest problem with these types of medication is that some people stop taking them abruptly. To suddenly stop taking these types of mood-stabilising medications is extremely dangerous. Under no circumstances should anyone who is taking these types of treatments stop taking them instantly. You will in no way hear me telling you to stop taking the medication. Are we clear? Let me explain. I firmly believe that people who have received faith in Christ should continue to take medication in Jesus' name while recovering. I know some don't agree with me. In fact probably the greatest push back I've received is from the small, and thankfully decreasing, numbers of people who think everything is solved with a single prayer. I feel greatly for this sector of the community and hope these words will bring comfort and genuine hope for the future. For the person of faith, taking medication while working through life's issues over a period of months or even years, your life will stabilise and grow to the point, that in many cases, the medication will gradually be reduced and eventually be removed. Medication needs to be seen as a part of the holistic approach to wellness.

It's true that some of the medications have side effects that are not nice. If medication reacts with you in ways that cause you anxiety, you should see your doctor, as quite often the first medication prescribed may not be the right one for you. Always remember that medication for the mind is not an exact science. Although great advances have been made in the understanding of different parts of the brain and its various areas and functions, our understanding is still in its infancy regarding the complexities of thought and emotion.

Of course, it's rare that someone enjoys taking medication. No one likes to take it, especially if they have faith. Medication and faith have been seen as two opposites and this is compounded if they believe that their mind should be instantly healed with a quick prayer.

Let us dispel the hyper-faith, condemnation-based philosophy that medication is evil. Even Jesus is known as our great physician, and the gospel writer, Luke, was a doctor. Wouldn't it be better to be thankful for our medical profession and learn to trust God and others through the times when we need medical advice? You may ask, what about this verse of scripture? "For God has not given us a spirit of fear; but of power, and of love, and of a sound mind." 2 Timothy 1:7 (KJV)[8]

Many Bible translations agree that the better translation for swfronismou[9] is 'self-discipline'[10] or 'self-control'[11] rather than 'sound mind.'[12] We can see a vast difference in how we can understand the scripture as a promise for us, especially if we are a sufferer of a mind that is not 'sound'.

Does God just zap us with a new 'sound mind' at the point of conversion or a prayer, or is it that the soundness of mind we so desire is actually obtained by 'self-discipline'?

---

8 The Holy Bible, King James Version. New York: American Bible Society: 1999 2 Timothy 1:7

9 The NKJV Greek English Interlinear New Testament. Thomas Nelson Publishers, Nashville. TN p.733

10 Holy Bible, *New International Version*, 1973, 1978, 1984, International Bible Society. Zonderzan Publishing House 2 Timothy 1:7

11 The NKJV Greek English Interlinear New Testament. Thomas Nelson Publishers, Nashville. TN p.733

12 The Holy Bible, *King James Version*. New York: American Bible Society: 1999; Bartleby.com, 2000

The zapping may seem easier and more desirable, yet self-discipline in the long run is much more beneficial. Let us relieve the pressure on all who take medication. I personally don't think God has a problem with it. We all need to just relax, breathe and progress forward in a guilt-free faith and encouragement-filled way toward complete holistic healing and restoration.

Very few would feel guilty for taking blood-thinning medication,

> *We all need to just relax, breathe and progress forward in a guilt-free faith and encouragement-filled way toward complete holistic healing and restoration.*

migraine tablets or for that matter, asthma medication. Why should there be such a stigma regarding mood stabilising medication? No one should feel guilty or in any way a lesser person just because they take medication to help the healing and recovery process.

MAKING HEADWAY

As we launch into the heart of this book, let us begin with the end in mind. What do we want to achieve by the process? How will we come to the conclusions that will cause us to take action and thus define our lives from this point forward?

Dr. Michael Merzenich, in his ground-breaking book 'Soft-Wired', writes; "It's also about making the best of every day, week, month, and year of your life - about having a better life at every age. It's never too early nor too late to redirect your life onto a personal path of greater growth and, if necessary, rejuvenation." [13]

It's never too late to make choices that can positively define our lives from this point forward.

As our aim is 'Winning between the Ears,' thus creating a state of wellness within our minds. Let us define wellness.

Wellness:

'To move toward greater health physically, mentally, emotionally and spiritually, thus producing a state of holistic wellbeing and reaching the fullness of our unique self.'

You will notice this definition begins with 'To move toward greater health.' This is key to our understanding, as wellness is not necessarily

---

[13] Michael Merzenich, Dr. *Soft-Wired. How the New Science of Brain Plasticity Can Change Your Life*. Parnassus Publishing, LLC San Francisco.

an achieved destination but rather a constant progressive movement in the right direction. Wellness today can always lead to greater wellness tomorrow. The mental capacity of an individual for instance is never stagnant. We either progress forward or we are digressing backwards.

> *Wellness is not necessarily an achieved destination but rather a constant progressive movement in the right direction.*

There are four key areas of wellness; physically, mentally, emotionally and spiritually. The lines between these four areas are crossed quite often. A well mind will automatically underpin our emotions. Our spiritual perceptions will influence our mental state and even lead to positive or negative change physically.

OUT OF CONTROL

The speed of life has accelerated exponentially over recent times. The culture and its expectations combined with the pace of life tend to dictate our way of living and trap us into a system of compliance. Even keeping up becomes a challenge. Merzenich writes: "It's not easy to keep up, when the brain is slowing down, and the world is spinning like a top."[14] Only a short few years ago if you walked down the street or ran into an acquaintance you would ask something like, "How are you going?", "What's up?", "Sup?" and so forth. The most common answer was something like "Good", "Fine", (even if they were lying), followed by, "How are you?" or something similar, depending on your location. If I were to ask you what you thought the number one answer to the question "How are you going?" is today, what would you say? "Yeah, busy." It seems that society never walks anymore and everything is at a frantic run. Lily Tomlin once quipped, "The trouble with the rat race is that even if you win, you're still a rat."[15]

---

14 Michael Merzenich, Dr. *Soft-Wired. How the New Science of Brain Plasticity Can Change Your Life*. Parnassus Publishing, LLC San Francisco.

15 Tomlin, Lily. BrainyQuote.com Rat Race Quotes. http://www.brainyquote.com/quotes/quotes/l/lilytomlin100013.html?src=t_rat_race (Accessed 29th November 2016)

OUT OF CONTROL

Many years ago a friend threw me the keys to his race tuned, fully worked Yamaha FJ1200 motorbike. With an engine four times larger than the bike I owned at the time, I ripped the throttle back and….Wow! It was one of those cartoon moments, where the person is gripping the bike and the rest of their body is flailing airborne behind. I was thankful for my full-face helmet, as I'm sure it stopped my eyes disappearing back into my skull. I was asked later, "How fast were you going?" My answer was, "I don't know, everything just flew past me in a blur." As much fun as that was, and it was fun, how many lives are lived at that pace today? The engine of life pulls us along so fast that life becomes a blur and we seem to be just hanging on. We can call it the blurring of life or the compression of time. Whatever it is, if your life is running frantically, then a revolution is in order. A revolutionary's mindset is this; 'I've had enough, something must be done.' I will do something to change this.'

One of society's great challenges today is the exponential increase in anxiety-related illness. 'Beyond Blue' published figures recently quoting the Mission Australia Youth Survey 2013. 'One in six young Australians is currently experiencing an anxiety condition and one in four young Australians currently has a mental health condition'.[16] These figures are alarming to say the least. I'm writing this book because I firmly believe that contained in these pages is a message and practical plan that can rescue thousands of lives. The increased speed of life, the false perfection bombardment from the media, and the alteration of our value markers have met in a perfect storm of anxiety on scales never witnessed before. As a result, we've even developed a medical condition peculiarly specific to 'western' fast paced nations called 'shallow breathing'. A heightened state of

---

16 Beyond Blue Depression. Anxiety. Stats and Facts. https://www.youthbeyondblue.com/footer/stats-and-facts (Accessed 29th November 2016)

tension is constant therefore our fight/flight centre of the brain designed to fire when needed, ends up firing constantly, flooding our body and mind with distress chemicals (Stress Hormones) and bodies/minds exposed to this over extended periods, begin to fail. But all is not lost.

CHOICE

In the 1980's - early 90's neuroscience went through a revolution. Conventional wisdom till this time believed that the neural pathways, once set were fixed or 'hard-wired.' Neural pathways establish the thought processes within our minds. Scientific thought, at the time, generally considered that these thinking pathways, genetically influenced and formed through the 'critical period' of childhood (new born till about eighteen months) became fixed and remained that way throughout maturity and adulthood. Science had known of changes to brain structure for many years prior to the discovery of Neuro-plasticity, yet the common perception was that the brain after puberty, only changed negatively toward gradual deterioration. The discovery that changed modern perceptions regarding our thoughts is that the brain can be rewired.

The term 'Neuro-plasticity' is used to explain the flexible, creative and re-creative way the mind can be altered. Granted, the more the brain ages and has entrenched and re-enforced pathways, the more challenging it is to rewire our thinking. We say of some older people,

*'The way we think is not by chance,
but by choice.'*

"You're set in your ways." Well yes, they are. They have well established neural pathways that they've run down so many times, forming well entrenched and strongly connected neural networks that are difficult to alter. Not only has the grass given way to the forest floor, there is now a trench or rut there as well. It becomes so deep some even get bogged there. For instance, if someone has spent 40 years believing they are of little value, whether as a result of unfortunate events in their childhood or broken relationships, failures or whatever, every thought regarding personal self-worth runs along this familiar yet faulty pathway. This results in situations where even a meeting with a successful individual that might motivate some, only proves to reinforce their personal lack of perceived value. Each time their thinking goes this way the synopsis strengthens bonds and the thinking becomes more ingrained. Another example would be a lady who considers herself not pretty enough. Her value markers may have been set by the airbrush-altered images bombarding her every day through the media. Therefore, as she looks in the mirror she only sees what's wrong and misses all the beauty that's truly there. We see this everywhere in our current culture. The value markers are so altered and so manufactured that it's impossible for all but a few, on their very best days, to even come close to that level of supposed perfection. Here's a thought; who gave the marketing firms the position of God? Why should they have the power to make me believe a lie about myself that I'm not good enough? I'm pretty passionate about this as I come across so many whose confidence and value is shattered by the proliferation of this false perfection. However, it is proven that no matter the age, rewiring is still achievable. It is now understood that new pathways can be created at any age.

'Most of all (the research) ... showed that the representation of the surfaces of the body in your brain and the wiring that sustained them are not cast in concrete. To the contrary, they were continually revisable. Not hard-wired; but soft-wired'.[17]

The brain is also wired by experience. The term EDP refers to 'Experience Dependent Neural-Plasticity.' This in laymen's terms means, we think a certain way because of the experiences we've been through. Therefore the experiences create how we think and perceive the world around us. Consider this; a child is born into this world with a natural tendency towards being academically gifted. This DNA bias we can refer to as 'nature'. Yet this same child grows up in a harsh critical and negative environment. This environment we refer to as 'nurture'. How the child is 'nurtured' will always trump how the child is by 'nature'. Their individual experience will create strong neurological pathways, thus EDP not only influences their lives but also creates habits that control their actions as well.

Even while reading about this you may think of people, places and circumstances that have profoundly affected your life. Thinking patterns, established through all life's various circumstances, should be considered in regard to Neural-Plasticity, and we should all be encouraged that at any age the brain can be re-written.

Being Dyslexic by 'nature' and compounded by failures (EDP) 'nurture', meant that my neural circuitry was well entrenched as destructive and negative, resulting in a lack of personal values and self-loathing. Habitual destructive behaviours developed around these beliefs in an attempt to simply survive life. So profound was my sense of worthlessness developed through both 'nature' and 'nurture' that I existed in constant despair. Some of these well-established neural pathways took years to overcome. I remember very early on in my faith journey, I'd be sitting in a gathering with about

---

17 Michael Merzenich, Dr. *Soft-Wired. How the New Science of Brain Plasticity Can Change Your Life.* Parnassus Publishing, LLC San Francisco.

sixty others when the minister would say something to the effect of, "Ok, we'll read the passage ..... together now, starting with dear sister Miriam up the back, and let's read a verse each working across the rows till we finish." Instantly, terror gripped me. There I was, 23 years old with the reading level of perhaps a struggling 10 year-old, many years of failure while trying to read in classes and the subsequent ridicule. So there I was, not wanting to look like an idiot and certainly not wanting anyone to know about my failings. Fear gripped me, survival mechanisms clicked in. Instinctively I counted every person who would read before me. I then worked my way to find the verse I would have to read. As the train came ever nearer, I would endeavour to find and read my one verse over a few times so I didn't mess it up and embarrass myself. I always hoped for 'Jesus wept' but never got it. Sure enough though, either dear sister..... or brother.... would get so excited they'd read a few verses and I'd be stuffed. Oh the stress of sitting in church! I laugh about it now but back then it was awful. By the way, we don't do that in our church anymore, thankfully.

Yet now I have had for years, a new 'nurture' environment. These disciplined reading programs and positive beliefs have not fully overcome the Dyslexic 'nature' but through constant rewiring of my mind, there has been significant improvement. This transformation for me becomes all the more clearer when I sit back and realise that this once school-dropout who struggled with 'Green Eggs and Ham,'[18] has a university degree, is an author, and travels, teaches, and even reads books on neuroscience. Crazy change, I know, and I do so love it 'Sam-I-am.'[19]

---

18 Dr. Seuss. *Green Eggs and Ham*. Beginner Books: Random House, 1960. New York, New York.

19 Ibid

BIBLICAL NEUROSCIENCE

So does modern scientific understanding stand at odds to ancient biblical teachings or do they actually correspond? I think they are so beautifully harmonized, they become like musical instruments coming together to create a philharmonic orchestra. Modern scientific discoveries have connected the dots of passages of scripture thousands of years old.

Looking at a few biblical texts, you can see how they relate to the re-wiring of the mind. Biblical Neuro-plasticity is a real thing. Within these ancient texts, written by various contributors over thousands of years, plasticity of the mind has always been a key to their fulfilment, not only in finding our unique self but living in all the fullness of what it means to be human. One school of thought would be that the entire New Testament challenges humanity to see all aspects of life, the universe and the value of people differently. Constantly Jesus (the greatest revolutionary of all) constantly challenged thinking. He would say things like, "You've heard it said" (Matt 5:21, 27, 31, 33, 38, 43[20]) ... then would state something of an old mindset. Then he'd say, "but I

---

[20] Holy Bible, *New International Version*, 1973, 1978, 1984, International Bible Society. Zonderzan Publishing House Matthew 5:21, 27, 31, 33, 38, 43

tell you.....[21]", always challenging perceptions and thought.

Let's take our first ancient text: "Do not conform any longer to the pattern of this world, but be transformed by the renewing of your mind."[22] This text has been around for over 2000 years. Think about this; if our neural pathways were fixed, then this piece of wisdom would make no sense, would it? Yet modern science brings this text into clearer focus. The dividing up of the text and using its original language sheds even greater light on the truth here. The word in the English language 'transformed' is translated from the ancient Greek 'metamorphousthe'[23] from which we obtain our English word 'metamorphosis.' This infers a transition, as going from one state through a process, 'a complete change of physical form or substance'[24] to become something completely new. 'It's this process of change or 'taking the new path to the river' that this passage is focusing on. In fact, a quick study of this New Testament letter to the Romans shows that the entire sixteen chapters pivot on this one verse. The development of a new way of thinking was as vital to the original hearers of this letter as they are to our society today. The word 'renewing' is from the same root word we use for 'renovation'.

If you've ever renovated a kitchen, a house, restored a car or any-

> *By changing the way we think, we create new neural pathways that transform our lives.*

---

21 Holy Bible, *New International Version*, 1973, 1978, 1984, International Bible Society. Zonderzan Publishing House Matthew 5:22, 28, 32, 34, 39, 44

22 Holy Bible, *New International Version*, 1973, 1978, 1984, International Bible Society. Zonderzan Publishing House Romans 12:2

23 The NKJV Greek English Interlinear New Testament. Thomas Nelson Publishers, Nashville. TN p.572

24 The Collins Paperback English Dictionary 1986 William Collins Sons & Co. Ltd. Glasgow G4 0NB p.531

thing like that, you'll know that it's never instant. In fact, you'll generally find most restorations or renovations take twice as long as desired and cost probably ten times what you expected. Therefore, we can read this ancient text in a fuller way like this; "Do not conform any longer to the pattern of this world, but go through a metamorphosis or renovation of our thinking to bring about a complete change for the better." In short, by changing the way we think, we create new neural pathways that transform our lives.

BUSY BRAIN

Around the age of 12 to18 months the human brain begins to settle into established neurological pathways. The brain then functions with around 100 billion neurons or brain cells for the rest of our lives. The human brain can perform approximately 30 billion processes per second, running along what is equivalent to about 8000 miles of cables/networks. There's a lot going on inside your head, isn't there? No wonder you're tired all the time!

It's interesting to note however, that during this early period a child has roughly three times the adult brain capacity. They're building the city they will live in for the rest of their lives using approximately 300 billion brain cells. So next time you're gooing and gaahing at a baby, remember, that baby has three times your brain cells. I know. Scary, right! The saving grace for adults is that the paths of the mind attributed to remembering our weird faces and sounds we make have not been established yet. We should all be thankful for this! Neuroscientist Dr. Michael Merzenich calls this early period the 'critical period... where the brain sets up the basic processing machinery'[25]. This is a great opportunity and an even greater responsibility to influence a child in ways that will influence the rest of their amazing lives. Dr. Wess Staf-

---

[25] Michael Merzenich, Dr. *Soft-Wired. How the New Science of Brain Plasticity Can Change Your Life*. Parnassus Publishing, LLC San Francisco.

ford, former president of Compassion International in his insightful book 'Too small to Ignore' states, "The spirit of a child is a lot like wet cement. When a child is young it takes little effort to make an impression that can last a lifetime."[26]

I'm guessing no one reading this book is less than 18 months old. If I'm correct then all of us have reached our location in life because of what was set in our early years and how we have adapted and

> *Although everything we've been through has led us to today, it's the choices we make today that will lead us into our tomorrows.*

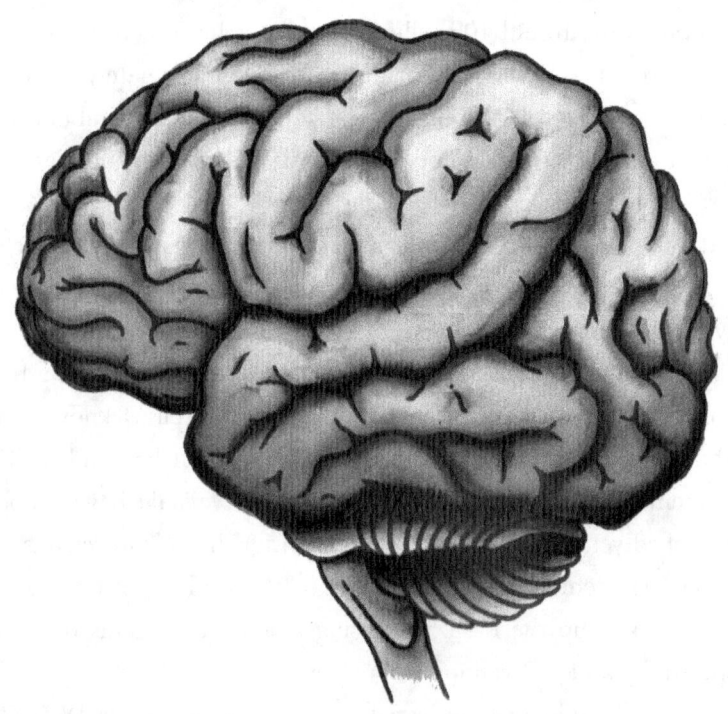

---

26 Stafford, Dr. Wess. *To Small To Ignore: Why the Least of These Matters Most.* Special Edition WaterBrook Press, Colorado Springs, Colorado p.9-10

rewired since that time. We are a blend of our 'critical period' as a child and of experiences (EDP) since then.

I know that while reading some of you may even feel pain or regret regarding your life. That's okay. You're certainly not alone in feeling this way and it's entirely normal. Always remember that although everything we've been through has led us to today, it's the choices we make today that will lead us into our tomorrows. Our early construction years and whatever twists and turns life has thrown at us since then, regardless of how long we've lived have all, the good, the bad and the ugly, done one very important thing. They have led us to right now. They have carried, dragged or pushed us to this important point, this pivotal moment in time. Although everyone would like to change some parts of their past, we cannot. Yet here is the beautiful thing. Although all our pasts have led us to who we are and what we've become right now, it's what we do today and from this day forward that will determine our future. The late Prime Minister of England, Winston Churchill, once stated, "Now this is not the end. It is not even the beginning of the end. But it is, perhaps, the end of the beginning."

Many years ago I began a sales career. I started door knocking on businesses with a bag of produces in one hand, and demonstration tools in the other. My territory comprised of an area no one else would do. It was extremely challenging. I remember after a particularly difficult day a wise old manager met me for breakfast, and knowing how challenging it had been said, "Do you know the best thing about yesterday?" (I could see nothing good in my yesterday).

I choose to live today and tomorrow,
and not yesterday over and over again.

He paused and continued, "It finished at twelve o'clock last night." So true! I know it's a little cliché but the truth remains that today is the first day of the rest of your life. I choose to live today and tomorrow, and not yesterday over and over again.

Years ago I self-published my first book called 'Life Beyond Mental Illness.' It was a raw, uncut version of what later became 'The Fog Lifter'. When I came out and started telling my story of depression, mental illness, attempted suicide and how through renewing the mind I now live free of mental illness, I decided to run a seminar. At this stage I didn't even know the term 'Neural-Plasticity' and had no concept of the areas of the brain and how they functioned. It was my first seminar. I was extremely nervous and truth be known it was not probably my greatest public speaking performance. Yet amongst the group that day was Jim. I'm not sure if I met Jim in person that day, but Jim later wrote to me several times. Diagnosed with Bi-Polar disorder, Jim had spent the last 25 years 'on the books' of the local mental health professionals. He was embedded within the mental health system and culture, but nothing was helping. I want to give you a sense of his life, because there are millions of 'Jims' around our world today. He was around the age of 40, had a traumatic childhood, broken relationships, out of work and unable to sustain regular employment. Add to that, heavily medicated, overweight, single, lonely and depressed. Jim's prospects were devoid of hope. Suicide was to him an ever-present voice. Fear in the present combined with regret of his past, and darkness enveloped his thoughts of the future. So Jim attends my seminar. Although he was unable to read a book at that stage, he decided to take some of the principles discussed and put them into action. In his own words he writes, "Since your seminar I have been going from strength to strength. Just recently Mental health in…. has discharged me from their system/books after being with them for 25 years." (June 2013)

Later he writes again saying, "I'm now doing a Cert III in Community Services and I've started helping others. Thank you. These principles have changed my life." (April 2015)

The past is already written - the future is not. Every person has hope for the future because every person has the ability to make choices today to influence their tomorrow. If you cannot see it at the moment, that's okay. Can I ask you to trust me on this one, simply because I've been there and I know? There are many other stories like Jim's. Stories of newfound hope, of futures restored, of personal transformation of the mind, spirit and soul. Everyone can be transformed. If you could have seen my life, the consuming hell it once was, and now how the fog has lifted and how bright it truly is, you would see clearly the result of a renewed mind.

New neural pathways now exist and rather than being controlled by my thoughts I now control my thoughts, and life flows from my new path to the river. The coolest thing is that this is for all. It will take time; it will take effort! Constructing healthy life-winning habits need to be formed and that's never instant, yet as this ancient Chinese proverb often attributed to Lao Tzu states, 'A journey of a thousand miles begins with one step'.[27]

> *The past is already written - the future is not. Every person has hope for the future because every person has the ability to make choices today to influence their tomorrow.*

---

[27] Tzu, Lao. Brainy Quotes.com Lao Tzu Quotes https://www.brainyquote.com/quotes/quotes/l/laotzu137141.html (Accessed February 28th 2017)

PEPPERONI

Learning Italian

So how do we begin changing our neurological pathways? Habits produce change neurologically. Once developed, a habit uses reinforcement to redefine our lives. So how do we begin?

Well the simple answer is that it all begins with an act of our will. Yet an act of will only becomes transformational once it becomes habitual, and this process takes time. Starting with an understanding and appreciation of process will liberate us to push through the struggles to achieve the mission of winning between the ears.

I have a friend who has taken the task of learning the Italian language. He's over 50 and is embarking on learning a new language. There are stages to learning a new language. Language expert Andrew Barr uses an aircraft taking flight metaphor: 'Take off, managing the bumps, gaining altitude and cruising'.[28] At first, learning a new language is difficult because your brain thinks in your native language. Existing neurological pathways are in place and have been strengthened over years of continued use. The native language within the mind's neural pathways is already defined. This is why the process

---

[28] Barr. Andrew, Fluent In 3 Months. The 4 Stages of Language Learning (And What to Do at Each Stage) http://www.fluentin3months.com/language-learning-stages/ (Accessed 29th November 2016)

PEPPERONI

is challenging. The brain actually doesn't want to change. It's happy with the current language because it can save time and energy defaulting to the existing wiring. New neural-pathways will never develop unless like getting the aeroplane off the ground, there is a tremendous amount of concentrated energy, intentionally applied in one direction. Thrust and aerodynamics must overcome gravity. Neural pathways will always gravitate in their established direction; therefore our thrust toward creating new pathways must be intentional. We require a focused direction and a commitment to the take off. I will use English as the base language simply because it's my native language.

When learning a new language, for example Italian, first you think in English, you translate to Italian, you speak in Italian, you hear the answer in Italian, and then convert the Italian to English so you can understand, then repeat the process. This all takes time and effort, yet the more you repeat the process the easier it becomes, till you reach the point where the new language becomes what we'd call 'integrated'. What's changed? Italian becomes fluent; you hear, understand and can respond easier - why? Neurologically speaking, you have created new mind pathways. You actually go from thinking in English to not just hearing in Italian, but actually thinking in the different language.

According to sociologist Dr. Ray Andrews, there are two things required to change your thinking; 'focused thought and repetition.'[29] In the example of learning a new language we see this is proven true through focused thought and repetition of action.

So, if it's possible to renew our minds by creating new neurological pathways, which it is, our first realization is that just like learning

---

29 Andrews Dr. Raymond New Life Worldwide Ministries. Advanced Workshop. Coffs Harbour Cex Club. September 2014.

a new language, it will take time. Although I like the idea of simply downloading the new knowledge onto my personal hard drive and all of a sudden be able to speak a new language, or think constantly on new and better pathways, it simply doesn't work that way. In the first Matrix movie, Trinity needed to know how to fly a helicopter so her team simply downloaded or uploaded the files into her mind. Wouldn't that be nice, but just like that movie was all about an alternate reality, if we think we can re-write our minds in a download, then we're living in our own little alternate reality. It's not how it works. It takes time, and generally more time than we wish. Yet, focused thought and repetition will always result in new pathways so let's get to it.

UP FRONTAL

We are extremely complex beings with the ability to transform our thinking. The design of the brain is a masterpiece. This essentially 80% watery, greyish mush is an astounding piece of engineering. Nicolaus Steno in 1669 said, "The brain, the masterpiece of creation, is almost unknown to us."[30] We've come a long way in understanding the brain since then, although the brain still contains many mysteries; for instance the origin of a thought is unknown, yet we have discovered much. The development of Functional Magnetic Resonance Imaging (fMRI) in the 1990's gave us insights into the brain like never before. Being able to track oxygen-rich blood flow in real time opened the window to seeing which parts of the brain were activated during various processes. Imaging has shown us what activates different sections of the brain and it is, in my opinion, one of the most fascinating and exciting areas of modern science. Simplistically, we can divide the brain into four 'Lobes'; the frontal, parietal, temporal and occipital lobes. In an endeavour to make the science of beginning brain renewal as simple as possible, I will for a short time, focus on the frontal lobe.

---

30 Head of Neuroscience. Neuroimaging and the art of personal Brain Manipulation. Ancient History of Neuroscience. http://headofscience.blogspot.com.au/2011/06/only-as-recently-as-past-few-decades.html (Accessed 28th November 2016)

Amongst the frontal lobes tasks are evaluation and judgment. This is where we analyse, come to conclusions and make subsequent choices based on the conclusions drawn from the analysis. In this process, we have the ability to decide whether a particular stimulus, for instance a thought, is constructive or destructive, whether it's harmful or helpful, healthy or unhealthy, whether it's truth or trash. Seeing how we are looking at the fact that we can control our thinking thus re-wiring our brains, this is our starting point. I am purposefully being simplistic here. What good is it, if our knowledge increases about the brain, yet it fails to translate into simple life altering actions? After all, the true measure of education is not information, but rather transformation. Therefore, as important as all the intricacies of the brain are, I find putting together a plan so clearly that I or anyone else can use it today, tomorrow, and every day, is far more important to the renewing of the mind. As I stated before, the brain

> *After all, the true measure of education is not information, but rather transformation.*

is an amazing piece of engineering and in my humble view it's something that can only be of divine origin. To me the brain, just like the universe, always points to intelligent design. You don't have to agree with me, but I would ask you to at the very least, let this be part of your consideration.

RIDING A HIPPO

The single greatest skill you will ever learn

I believe learning to control the thought life is the single greatest skill any human being can ever develop. Every outside stimuli that requires our decision making process, finds its way into the frontal lobe. Past information is stored as layered memories in our hippocampus. 'The hippocampus plays a critical role in the formation, organisation, and storage of new memories as well as connecting certain sensations and emotions to these memories.'[31] When a decision is required, the past information stored mainly in the hippocampus connects to the frontal lobe and we seem to know what choice to make because of stored information. We instinctively know not to place our hand in a fire because stored information informs us that it will hurt. We quite often don't even think about it, as our shortcut preference oriented mind already knows it's not a wise thing to do.

However, we often make choices or subconsciously accept even wrong thoughts because they identify with our layered memories and core beliefs. Out of our layered memories we draw our core belief systems and from our core beliefs emerges our identity. So many of these choices we don't even consider properly. If our core belief is faulty and

---

31 Very Well. What is the Role of the Hippocampus? https://www.verywell.com/what-is-the-hippocampus-2795231 accessed April 4th 2016

we see ourselves negatively, then we mostly accept negative outside stimuli without hesitation or conscious thought. The importance of not just accepting random thoughts but rather bringing them into the conscious decision making process within the frontal lobe, is essential in re-wiring our minds.

For instance: What if all my life I have felt I was of little worth. This was huge for me personally. As a very sick child, chronic asthmatic and Dyslexic, I developed a powerful sense of dislike for myself. Each failure to read, embarrassing mistakes and hospital trips added to my layered memories. I had, stored in my hippocampus, well developed layered memories informing and reinforcing my core belief, even though it was false, and out of this, my crippled identity was formed.

Have you considered this; belief is more powerful then truth. Therefore, the true power to live the greatest life we can live comes when we connect truth and belief and let this form our identity. It is my desire that you learn to pull everything you may have accepted about yourself out of the subconscious and into the conscious mind and make decisions based on truth, not perception. Stephen Covey stated, "We see the world, not as it is, but as we are."[32] This is the starting point of mind renewal. It's the first step in starting on the new path to the river, forming new neural circuitry and thus obtain-

> *The importance of not just accepting random thoughts but rather bringing them into the conscious decision making process within the frontal lobe, is essential in re-wiring our minds.*

---

[32] Covey. Stephen R. The 7 Habits of Highly Effective People: Powerful Lessons in Personal Change. FranklinCovey Co, 2012

ing a healthy identity. The habits that will transform your life begin with repeated conscious choices.

ACCESSORISING

The greatest of all fashion accessories

Let's connect the ideas around biblical neuroscience to an ancient society. Within the ancient Jewish culture people could be seen wearing the greatest fashion accessory of all time. Even today many Israelites still wear these when going to pray. They look weird to non-Jewish people like me. They are little boxes worn on their head and arm. They're called Phylacteries or Tefillin. Thousands of years ago, their God spoke to the Jewish nation saying, "Fix these words of mine (God's words) in your hearts and minds; tie them as symbols on your hands and bind them on your foreheads."[33] This ancient piece of wisdom speaks of the importance of placing God's words over the heart and as close as possible to your mind. The obvious question to this would be, why?

The Jewish interpretation of the above passage led to the creation of what I have loosely termed 'fashion accessories,' although fashion is really not what this is about. There is a genuine life changing understanding attached to these little boxes and if we can fashion this truth to our lives it can revolutionise our thinking. The boxes are hollow and there are two in the set. Without going into the manufacturing process,

---

33 Holy Bible, *New International Version*, 1973, 1978, 1984, International Bible Society. Zonderzan Publishing House Deuteronomy 11:18

leather from kosher cows and all the other intricacies, let's look at a simple, profound and powerful truth here. The text here is: 'Fix these words of mine in your hearts and minds; tie them as symbols on your hands and bind them on your foreheads.'[34] One box is strapped to the inside of the left arm and sits as close to the heart as possible. Inside these boxes are small hand written scrolls filled with significant promises or statements from biblical text. The straps are then wound around the arm finishing tied around the middle finger, thus fulfilling this verse in having God's words near your heart and tied as symbols on your hands. Although the box is designed to be fixed as close as possible to the physical heart, it's the understanding that 'the

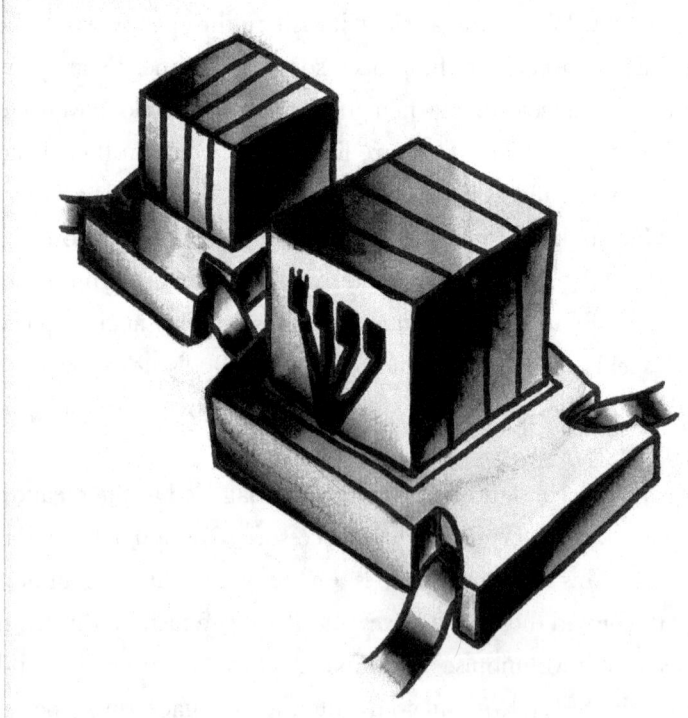

34 Ibid Deuteronomy 11:18

heart' is considered the centre of our being and the essence of our life. The heart is what causes life to flow through our being, and is often referred to as the place of the soul. Yet the boxes themselves are not the important part of this process. Inside the boxes are small hand written scrolls with promises God has made to His people. These are 'God's promises' re-written by hand and placed within these Phylacteries. The second box contains God's promises as well. This is the one I find most interesting. The plan is to look after not only the heart, but also the head by attaching God's truths as a person's point of reference in their lives. This exercise attaches absolute truths of God, physically close to the natural organs of the heart and brain and symbolizes the spiritual exercise of having God's truth covering the heart and mind. It has been said, "Above all else, guard your heart, for it is the wellspring of life"[35] Proverbs 4:23. There is truth here, but let me say this, if we don't protect our head (our thoughts) we'll never protect our heart, for what travels through the mind plants and grows in the heart. It is vital to guard your heart as everything in life flows from it, yet we cannot guard our hearts if we don't guard our heads. For our thoughts produce a crop of core values from which our identity grows, which is our heart's true condition. If we guard our head, we protect our heart.

Therefore, if 'above all else' we are determined to guard our heart, the most critical protection point is the gate of our minds. How then do we guard our head? That's a billion-dollar question. The placement of the second Phylactery is directly on the forehead. Consider this; in the days this was written, science had not discovered what sections of the brain did what. There was no thermal imaging, magnetic resonance imaging, CT scanning, electromagnet-

---

[35] Holy Bible, *New International Version*, 1973, 1978, 1984, International Bible Society. Zonderzan Publishing House Proverbs 4:23

ic or other scanning techniques. So consider where it sits. Isn't it interesting that it's right over the frontal lobe, which is our analysis, evaluation and decision making centre. God's desire is to have what he says about us as our point of reference over the decision making centre of our lives. This life changing understanding is that if we will let our evaluation and decision centre of our brain be governed by God's promises rather than our hurts, hassles, hang-ups and past layered memories, then we shall make choices that guard out minds and will automatically guard our hearts. You might say that's a nice theory, but how does it play out practically?

When you're hiking a compass will always give you true north. This way we can travel any direction because we know a definite point. Our culture is always screaming at us and the voices seem endless and loud, yet we can navigate life with far more assurance when we know where true north is.

I know you're probably not likely to order a set of Phylacteries and wear them on your next public outing. Granted, they would be a great conversation starter. Although I would not wear them either, every day I must walk through my life with whatever it holds for me the good, the bad and the ugly. Literal boxes or not, to live the greatest life of all, filled with joy, peace, hope and truth, I must be equipped with the revelation of God's promises over my mind. In a world where we are constantly bombarded with voices, where the propaganda of our culture constantly infers I don't measure up to this false perfection, it is vital to have the statements God has written about me plastered all over my thinking process for it's only then I can make my life's choices accurately.

Sub it out

Real life change comes through constantly choosing, consciously, one

thought at a time. Yes, it's difficult at first to trust and believe God's words concerning me over my past-layered memories that have established my core belief and identity. Yet it's within these choices we set in motion the process of reforming our minds in order to create a new and true identity. Granted, if your understanding of God is based around some messed up concept of who He is, then that's the place to start. For instance, if my concept of God is that He's sitting on some cloud with a giant lightning bolt in hand, waiting for me to stuff up so He can take me out, well that's pretty messed up anyway, and I wouldn't want that idea dominating my frontal lobe thank you. However, I've found the truth of God's love and His value placed on all humanity, astounding. Therefore, armed with images of grace, love, joy and peace and allowing them to occupy my evaluation and decision-making centre, my choices and subsequently my life will be transformed. That's why they are placed on the frontal lobe. The only answer for wayward or faulty thinking is creating new neurological pathways through choice-orientated, repetitive correct thinking.

Defined
We are not defined by our thoughts, but rather what we do with our thoughts is what will define us.
The truth that I am not defined by my uncontrolled thoughts took me a long time to understand. Even as a believer I struggled with this one. I thought that because I had bad thoughts, that meant I was a bad person. As I had spent six years mentally ill, my mind was plagued with what I'd now call 'stinkin' thinkin'.' My mind was still taking its broken and destructive layered memories as truth, and accepting habitual thoughts that were simply not true. Twenty-three years of habitually thinking incorrectly meant well defined neurological pathways that unless consciously altered, would never change. Without alluding to particular types of thoughts that would run riot and mess me up, to say I needed a 'check up from the neck up' would be an extreme understatement.

It was not till I realised that the power is not in the thought itself, but rather in the accepting or rejecting of the thought. The statement that: 'I really cannot choose what thoughts I have' is true yet also untrue. Although we are all subject to random thoughts and the origin of a thought is not fully understood, the constant renewal of the mind will lead to far better thinking processes and in turn better random thoughts. I can choose what I do with the thoughts I have. In the

> ***The power is not in the thought itself, but rather in the accepting or rejecting of the thought.***

ACCESSORISING

process of choosing what to do with my thoughts, I will over time, change the foundation of my thinking. This changes my core belief system and therefore my identity. Once achieved, even random thoughts become better as they flow from a healthier mindset. This does not mean I am devoid of random, wrong thoughts. Yet in comparison to the dominance destructive thinking once had over me, wrong thoughts are certainly infrequent now. Why? Because over time neural plasticity has proven true and new pathways are developed, leading to new-layered memories, a new set of core beliefs and a new identity. The mind will adapt and reinforce neurologically to what it deems best for itself.

During the critical period (new born to 18 months) the brain is constructing massive networks or pathways and these are being formed and strengthened by the environment around the child. Yet from the late teens or even earlier, till life's end, a human being and thus a human mind can strategically, beginning with an act of its will creating habits, choose to alter its own configuration. The mind, will however only do this when it perceives personal benefit. Merzenich writes: "…the older brain allows change to occur specifically when it determines, by its own standards, that change would be good for it."[36] We all have random thoughts, some people more than others, but that is not the point. It's the control over the thoughts that makes the difference. Understanding 'like produces like' is fundamental to brain renewal. A neurological pathway is defined by repetition and focused thought and strengthened through usage.

This is why negative thinking will always promote more negative thinking, because continual usage strengthens the synapses and insulates the pathways making them stronger and more resistant to

---

36 Michael Merzenich, *Dr. Soft-Wired. How the New Science of Brain Plasticity Can Change Your Life*. Parnassus Publishing, LLC San Francisco. page 47 –Kindle EBook

change. It works this way negatively, yet thankfully it works the same way positively. Although it can take considerable time to convert a negative mindset into a positive one, it all comes down to the way we choose to direct our thoughts. The battle for the mind is always won, one thought at a time. So how do we accomplish control of our thoughts and achieve brain renewal?

BUBBLE

A thought comes in - what's next?

Here comes a thought. It will be either positive or negative. It may be neutral, however we will focus around the negative and positive and their long-term results. So, it (the thought) arrives in our frontal lobe. Here comes the skill part; instead of accepting that thought blindly we capture the thought. This is possible, even if the thought identifies with our previous layered memories. This is choosing to take an unconscious decision process and deciding to consciously choose to accept or reject differing thoughts. I'm not talking about habitual behaviours like indicating when turning left while driving. Not that indicating when turning isn't important; I'm more concerned about the thoughts that would affect our self-worth and be either destructive or constructive towards our core beliefs and outworking within our identity. If we use the driving metaphor, some of us have accepted habitual thoughts about others and ourselves for so long, we need to learn to drive again. We can, and in essence, must stop the thought in our frontal lobe, as it's there that we as individuals can make a conscious choice to accept or reject a thought. Here is another piece of wisdom that has proven true over time. It is something that has saved my life many thousands of times and is foundational in producing a new and sound mind. Scripture states, "We take captive every thought...".[37] The language used here is military by nature. Science has proven we can through the act of our will and the analyzing and decision-making faculty within our frontal lobe, capture our thoughts. The imagery in this passage is that of dragging a captive enemy away in chains.

If you want better thinking it will not just happen. As good as praying is, a mind will not be renewed instantly. This may mess with some people's theology. So be it. It takes intentionality, determination, repetition and focus. Habitual destructive thoughts need to be treated for what they are. Enemies to your life! This is not a passive approach at all. This is an aggressive approach to wrong thinking. To control your thought life you need a military mindset. This is a stra-

> *We will either control our thoughts or our thoughts will control us.*

tegic military mindset of a conquering revolutionary army. This is no half-baked, touchy feely 'it would be nice if it all worked out' thing. We have to overthrow the current governing authorities of our mind. The only way to do that is a revolution. If a negative thought tells me I'm no good, I owe it to myself, my soul, my life, my future and the lives of all I know and influence, to take that false thought captive, drag it away and shoot the sucker. I know that flies directly in the face of our western politically correct passivity. If your mind has caused you distress and you've believed wrong thoughts, perhaps lies about yourself and others, then there is a time and the time is now to bring those thoughts into captivity. This must become a revelation to you for this revolution to succeed! It's the conscious choice

---

37 Holy Bible, *New International Version*, 1973, 1978, 1984, International Bible Society. Zonderzan Publishing House 2 Corinthians 10:5

to capture thoughts and decide to accept or reject them that will in time create the habit that will change everything in your world. Think of a holding cell. The police pick up someone suspected of being in the wrong. They place them in a holding cell. Then they weigh up the evidence, the person is then either arrested or released. This is exactly how we are to examine our thoughts. A thought comes in like this; 'you're amazing and loved'. I take that thought captive. It's true, therefore I accept that thought and let it go from my head to my heart, and my life is enhanced with my core belief and identity growing from this truth. The process repeated over time creates new layered memories stored in my Hippocampus and from those layered memories my core values and identity are formed and re-formed. That is a positive example, however most people battle with the direct opposite. A thought comes in like; "I'm not good enough" or "I'm worthless, I've messed up my life" or "Who could ever love me" and so forth. So here is what we must do with these thoughts, we choose to choose what to do with these thoughts by putting them in the holding cell. Even though wrong thinking may seem right because our established pathways agree, these negative thoughts are actually false and destructive. Are we going to fiddle and play around with them till they destroy our lives? Are we going to continually simply accept lies as truth? We will either control our thoughts or our thoughts will control us. Make no mistake. I believe in capital punishment for destructive thoughts! Aggressive repeated determined action. There is a warning regarding this: Destructive thought patterns will resist and resurrect again and again, but eventually they will be subdued as they are replaced with correct thinking. Eventually new and healthy positive neural pathways will establish. These will produce better habitual thoughts and it will become easier to identify and take action upon any destructive thought.

Here's a question for you; what do we do with trash? We put the trash in the bin - don't we? That's precisely what we must consciously do. Put the trash in the bin! During this process you will be replacing the negative with a positive, thus laying down new memories based around a new set of beliefs and in the process creating new neural pathways producing a new and healthy life.

Someone once said, "You cannot control birds flying over your head, but you can stop them building their nest in your hair."

Remember, it's not the thoughts that define us. Oh, I used to believe this and it almost destroyed me. As I said, I would have thoughts come in from left field and I'd feel so guilty and ashamed. I thought because I had an evil thought, therefore I must be evil. Not true!

Everybody has thoughts. What define us are not the thoughts we have, but rather what we do with the thoughts we have. Even as a young preacher, not knowing how to control my thoughts shattered me, time and time again. I would preach and see great things happen. Lives were lifted and transformed by God's word and people encouraged, yet within an hour I could have a suicidal thought. I know that messes with some people's theology and I also realise that to grasp the greater picture fully, one would have to know how mentally ill I was before this time. I knew my past was forgiven. I knew I was a new creation. I was not half-baked or involved in some secret evil dealings. I was just a young man who had been very ill and was beginning a renewal process. These thoughts would crush me and I'd spent extended time riddled with guilt, till I learnt the greatest skill of all, in how to control my thinking. This transformed my life and it will transform yours also. Capturing our thoughts and dealing

> ***What define us are not the thoughts we have,***
> ***but rather what we do with the thoughts we have.***

BUBBLE

with them accordingly changes everything, and I literally owe my life to this conscious capturing of thoughts process. Doing this is so much easier now. I have the odd random thought now that I simply scoff and tell to get lost because my identity identifies it easily for what it is. It's a habit now, to bin rubbish thinking and quickly move on.

Let's just examine back a few verses from the passage we quoted before regarding, 'bringing every thought into captivity'[38].

2 Cor 10:3-5 NIV

3 For though we live in the world, we do not wage war as the world does. 4 The weapons we fight with are not the weapons of the world. On the contrary, they have divine power to demolish strongholds. 5 We demolish arguments and every pretension that sets itself up against the knowledge of God, and we take captive every thought to make it obedient to Christ.

I want you to look at the language here. You will notice the mil-

---

[38] Holy Bible, *New International Version*, 1973, 1978, 1984, International Bible Society. Zonderzan Publishing House 2 Corinthians 10:5

itary tone of how this is written. This connection is very important. Think about this: If ever since I can remember I have seen myself as a failure or somehow not good enough and not measuring up, then that's where I form my identity from. I have layer upon layer of memories that reinforce this misconception and therefore it becomes a natural thing to accept thoughts that agree with the layered memories I already have. Therefore I must intentionally re-layer the memories stored in my hippocampus with a correct understanding, then repeatedly re-layer new memories over the old and in the process I will automatically change my identity. This is where the new point of reference comes in. We need to change the point of reference. God asked His people to put what He says about them on their frontal lobes. This is so, when we capture and make decisions regarding our thoughts. The point of reference we use is what God says over our lives, not what our past and all its various experiences and traumas may say. For instance, if my past says I'm no good, yet God's promises say that, I'm valued and loved, these are opposites, aren't they? Real freedom comes from believing what God speaks regarding each of us, not what our past, the media or culture dictates to us.

So here is where I believe the 'divine power to demolish strongholds' comes in. An uncontrolled thought life is a stronghold, and a stronghold by nature is a fortified military installation. It takes great determination, willpower, intentionality, strategic planning and resolve to conquer a stronghold. There is a price to pay for this victory. This is the reason for the military mindset and the terminology used

> *Real freedom comes from believing what God speaks regarding each of us, not what our past, the media or culture dictates to us.*

in this passage. This is why I speak of revolution, because if your mind has held you captive for years it will take powerful determination connected to divine weaponry to overcome and be victorious! It will take battle after battle, repeated forays against the enemy's fortified strongholds. Yet my friends, continued commitment and constant courage will overcome those strongholds and the sweetness of victory will be achieved. It is something to be savoured and enjoyed always. The battle is worth the cost. It's worth any price, as victory is worth fighting for. For as Sir Winston Churchill once put it, "Without victory, there is no survival".[39] Is not this entire process all about freedom? Freedom to live life to the full. Freedom as an eagle to soar on the heights and not be locked in the cages of our minds. This is true freedom.

In verse five of this passage we read, "We demolish arguments and every pretension that sets itself up against the knowledge of God, and we take captive every thought to make it obedient to Christ." Think about this for a moment. If our thoughts dominate us in a negative framework regarding who we are or the state of things around us, then our thoughts are based around our past perceptions and established neural-pathways. These can be false 'arguments and pretensions'. These then set themselves up against the knowledge of God. What does 'against the knowledge of God mean'? It means false thinking sets itself as an enemy or as an armed opposing force against the truth of how God sees us. These false thoughts say things contrary to what God says about you. These are warring parties - aren't they? We know this. We know that if we win the battle between the ears we will have a greater life. This is why it's so important to get this right. Do you ever feel at war in your

---

[39] The International Churchill Society. Blood, Toil, Tears and Seat. http://www.winstonchurchill.org/resources/speeches/1940-the-finest-hour/blood-toil-tears-and-sweat (Accessed 5th December 2016)

mind? The 'divine power' comes when we bring every thought into captivity and make it obedient to Christ. 'Make it obedient to Christ' is an interesting phrase so let us explore it for a moment. To make a thought obedient to Christ is to literally compare the thought to what Christ speaks over our lives. Remember the holding cell idea, then analysing what's truth versus what's trash. All truth will connect to what God speaks positively over your life. Doing this often enough produces new neural-pathways, thus rewiring the brain and changing our lives completely.

NORTH

**The ability of the frontal lobe to decide.
Your True North.**

As a compass is only useful when it defines north correctly, so within our mind a well-defined and real 'True North' is vital. This is why we need a new 'True North'. The benefit is that you may go South, East, West or anywhere in between, as long as we know where North is first. The only way you can know where South exists is by knowing where North is. It's the setting of North that makes it possible to achieve our destination. When it's morning we can tell where East is. In the evening we can tell where West is, naturally. Yet it's in the blackness of midnight when our thoughts turn us around and around making it easy to be disorientated. Knowing our True North will make all the difference. The challenge comes in many lives when the setting of the mind is faulty through upbringing, past trauma and believing things false about themselves. The mind will always take the established North or the existing neural pathways, into account. In my case it all started to change when I began believing what God said over my life. I decided to make this as my new true North. One ancient king navigated 'the valley of the shadow of death'[40] by relying and focus-

---

[40] Holy Bible, *New International Version*, 1973, 1978, 1984, International Bible Society. Zonderzan Publishing House Psalm 23:4

ing his thoughts on what he knew to be true, rather than the visible signs from his current situation. By doing this we can navigate safely through the foggiest days and the darkest of nights.

NAPOLEON

"You cannot conquer until you replace"
- Napoleon[41]

"If you do not conquer self, you will be conquered by self."
-Napoleon Hill[42]

"The first and greatest victory is to conquer yourself;
to be conquered by yourself is of all things most shameful and vile."
- Plato[43]

"Subdue your appetites, my dears,
and you've conquered human nature."
- Charles Dickens[44]

---

41 Accredited to Napoleon: Andrews Dr. Raymond New Life Worldwide Ministries. Advanced Workshop. Coffs Harbour Cex Club. September 2014.

42 Happy Publishing. 61 Self-Control Quotes That Can Change Your Life https://www.happypublishing.com/blog/self-control-quotes/ (Accessed February 28th 2017)

43 Plato. Brainy Quotes Conquered Quotes. https://www.brainyquote.com/quotes/quotes/p/plato108514.html?src=t_conquered (Accessed February 28th 2017

44 Dickens, Charles. Brainy Quotes Conquered Quotes. https://www.brainyquote.com/quotes/quotes/c/charlesdic383675.html?src=t_conquered (Accessed February 28th 2017)

WINNING BETWEEN THE EARS

We can only finally defeat wrong thinking with right thinking. Napoleon stated that you cannot conquer until you replace. Naturally speaking, if you do not replace the governing authorities, the current systems and a large portion of the influential people, then the revolution will fail and the nation will automatically revert to its recognized establishments. Nations do this; minds do this. It is always easier to walk down a well-trodden path. A revolution of our thinking must be committed, continual and seen through, till new neural pathways are created and re-enforced. The governing authorities of our minds must be overthrown by a new way of thinking. Within our mind, as we replace our past thinking with better newer thinking, we start the process of re-layering of memories and producing a more positive set of core values and ultimately a transformed identity.

The Apostle Paul within the closing remarks of his letter to the church in Philippi, expresses some great wisdom. This wisdom has

"You cannot conquer until you replace" - Napoleon

helped millions over the years and continues to be a profound influence in lives today. This thought is found in all modern mental health procedures, all techniques from CBT (Cognitive behavioral therapy) to 'mindfulness', and other thought controlling techniques.

It says this:

Phil 4:8-9 NIV 8 "Finally,...whatever is true, whatever is noble, whatever is right, whatever is pure, whatever is lovely, whatever is admirable—if anything is excellent or praiseworthy—think about such things. 9 Whatever you have learned or received or heard from me, or seen in me—put it into practice. And the God of peace will be with you."[45]

I know what it is like to live a great deal of my life without peace, where fear controlled and consumed every waking hour. Yet now peace rules and I have learnt that it's so transformational to take these words and let them be my point of choice, thus becoming the reference point for my frontal lobe decisions. It works, it's true, and this truth truly does set you free.

CBT

Although I'm personally a huge fan of CBT, one of the limitations to Cognitive Behavioral Therapy (CBT) has always been the fact that unless a person's fundamental belief about who they truly are changes, then positive thinking and controlling the thoughts will always have limited results and a high rate of regression. This is due to the fact that if the core belief is faulty and doesn't change, then eventually the subject will always regress back to the same old path to the river.

In one of my past workplaces I was a sales trainer for a large fortune 500 Company. With a multicultural sales force, I trained all types of people from various backgrounds. I learnt what was far more important than the training process was the person's individual core belief. I watched how seemingly talented, sharp and gifted individuals would fall short, trip themselves up and eventually, even if they reached some level of success, it was never the level they could have attained. While observing this, I also noted that we could take a raw recruit who seemed less talented, struggled with the language and had many other reasons not to succeed, and they would flourish and go on to produce a great career. The key was not the training, al-

---

[45] Holy Bible, *New International Version*, 1973, 1978, 1984, International Bible Society. Zonderzan Publishing House Philippians 4:8-9

though as the trainer I'd say it was excellent! The key was not natural talent or giftedness or opportunity. The key was personal core belief.

Here's what I know; if your core belief is that you are of little worth, then no matter the positive reinforcement I give you, there will always be an acceptance of destructive thoughts that connect with pour a self-image.

Therefore I want to talk about your value. Not your investment portfolio, your cash assets, property or stocks. I want to discuss your core value, what you really believe about yourself. I will be very open and vulnerable here because this was a personal battle that took me a long time to win. As I've travelled and spoken in many and varied places, the personal value issue constantly comes to the fore as one of the biggest difficulties facing people.

COOL RUNNIN'S MAN

The movie 'Cool Runnings'[46] is a classic comedy based on a true story. Hopefully you have seen this movie, if not, stop everything and see it if you can!

If you've seen this movie, you may remember how 'Cool Runnings' is based on the incredible story of the Jamaican bobsled team going to the winter Olympics in Calgary, Canada in 1988. The team's coach, played by John Candy, is a disgraced great of the sport who was found cheating and subsequently lost all his Olympic medals. There's a powerful and profound moment in the movie where he (John Candy) is talking to the bobsled driver and leader of the young Jamaican team.

It's the night before the gold medal run, and although they were treated as outsiders and mocked in the beginning, they had proven themselves and stood a chance of a medal. In his room, preparing for the gold medal run the next day, young Doreas asked the coach why he cheated. Candy, after describing how he had made winning his whole life and how he had to win at all costs, makes this statement. "… a gold medal is a wonderful thing. But if you're not enough without it, you'll never be enough with it."[47]

---

46 *Cool Runnings*. Directed by Jon Turteltaub. Walt Disney Pictures. 1993

47 Ibid

Success and achievement is like that. It's a wonderful thing! But if we are not enough without it, we will never be enough with it. If our value is based in our accomplishments or our wealth, then what happens if our wealth vanishes and our accomplishments fail? Why do many who have achieved great things still fall into depression and mental illness? Why do seemingly successful people destroy relationships or live in a state of despair year after year?

Success is good, and achieving certainly is desirable over under or non-achieving, but it's not the key to a successful life. I think we should always aspire to living bigger lives, doing better and being brighter. It's a good thing. It is however like that gold medal. "It's a wonderful thing," but "if you're not enough without it, you'll never be enough with it."

I grew up in Sydney Australia at a time when wealth was considered everything. You already know that I was a very sick child, struggled with dyslexia at a time when there was little known about it and certainly was not catered for in the school system. I viewed myself as a person of little worth. By my teen years I had a well-developed destructive poor self-image. I endeavoured to then prove I was of worth by determining to become wealthy, after all that was where the promise of happiness lay. So I went after it. I set out to become rich. For some reason the more successful I became, the emptier I felt. Success meant I could fake being of value to those around me. If you knew me then and we were perhaps at a party together, you could have thought I had it all together and was successful and happy, you could have even considered that I was the life of the party. Yet I was miserable, hurting, troubled, paranoid, suicidal, and faking everything in order to cover how I really viewed myself - as worthless.

After going through all the craziness of my late teens and early twenties, the bad behaviour, the suicide attempt, the breakdown, the hospitals, the location moves and everything else, after all that, I became a Christ follower. I clearly remember telling my little brother that I became a Christian and his exact response was, "Well, you needed it." He was right! There was nothing low key about my conversion. I was overwhelmingly lost and broken. I knew that the deepest parts of hell awaited me and frankly believed I deserved them. Yet, on that night, at a youth camp in Tallebudgera near the Gold Coast, Queensland, I had my life radically changed. I knew I was changed. Till that point I lived in constant and at times, consuming fear. My fear collided with perfect love that day and I have never had a paranoid episode since. This is my story and we all have different stories and are at differing places on the journey to life and faith. I wanted to tell you this because I can use this background to illustrate this whole question of value. I knew I was changed. I knew I had received a new start to life and a great and supernatural joy flowed from that moment. Those at the camp said I hugged everything. If it moved I hugged it. So filled with joy was I that I even hugged Robyn, who would become my wife a couple of years later. I hugged so many people; I was probably embarrassing to be around. The drunk on the street corner, people I'd never met before, even the passing Labrador. It moved; I hugged it! I don't however remember hugging Robyn. I have a complete blank on that one. So how's that. I actually cannot remember the first time I hugged my future wife, and she doesn't let me forget it. My conversion was a life-changing evening, yet deep down; my core beliefs that grew from my layered memories were set like concrete. I was spiritually renewed yet neurologically, basically unaltered. I still saw myself of little worth. Therefore, because this core belief needed changing, it hindered my progress in renewing my mind. Why? Because I still accepted and believed thoughts that were unhealthy and untrue, based on existing neural pathways.

As a very new believer, my mind would still run wild. Two, three, four in the morning, I would be awake. Thoughts would run rampant. Although fear had gone, my mind was still broken. A wise older guy gave me the greatest advice you can ever give someone. I still remember it clearly. He walked up to me on a building site. Firstly, he told me everything about building the house I was working on, then simply, yet with eyes that drilled into my soul, looked at me and said, "Listen son, you gotta get the Word of God into ya." He had no idea I couldn't read! He did not know the trouble my mind would cause me through the nights. Someone gave me a King James Bible as a gift. It was a lovely gift, but the only problem was I literally could not read it. Thankfully someone helped me and gave me a more readable version. I would sit in a little one bedroom converted garage under a house in Coffs Harbour during the night with my ruler. I would place the ruler on one line and read it, sometimes over and over again. Not always on purpose either. Yet as I did this, night after night I started to discover things. I discovered that I was created by God for God and He loves me just the way I am. This blew my mind. You mean to say I'm not an accident after all! I discovered that I was 'fearfully and wonderfully made'[48], that I could be surrounded by darkness, yet that darkness 'is as light to Him'[49]. I discovered that His fingerprints are all over my DNA and He knows my comings and goings. To think, as mind boggling as it was to me, that in those early hours of the morning, in the midst of all my turmoil and destructive thinking, He knew it and still loved me. He knew my thoughts, as wicked as they were at times, and He still loved me. He knew my ups and downs, my good days and bad days. I discovered that He

---

48 Holy Bible, *New International Version*, 1973, 1978, 1984, International Bible Society. Zonderzan Publishing House Psalm 139:14

49 Ibid Psalm 139:12

even saw my unformed body and knitted me together to be me. This to a young man who thought he was 'behind the door' when the brains were handed out, enabled me to discover that nothing could separate me from Him. No height or depth, nothing at all. All this because of the bond created from that night in Tallebudgera.

There is this little statement that most probably skips over in Psalm 139. In those dark hours, lost in thoughts, from years of mental turmoil and feeling that I was alone, eight small words impacted me profoundly. These eight words may not have meant very much to many people, but for someone who knew the emptiness, loneliness and black hours like I did, these words became an anchor within my turbulent sea and I guess the first promise I placed on my forehead; 'When I awake, I am still with you.' To know that even in the loneliness of the night I was actually not alone was for me, life altering. Years later three small verses changed my life. Please indulge me with this, as I know this to be true. These verses, although they're my life verses, the axis my world turns on, if you get them or really let them 'get you', they will change you forever. I think I battled with my self-worth for about 10 years after becoming a Christ follower. Then through a set of circumstances too long to expound here, circumstances that included the death of my younger brother, having sickness almost take one of my daughters and all manner of other things that drove me to despair, these three small verses changed my life.

There is a chapter in the gospel according to Luke that tells three stories. The stories are of a lost sheep and a sheep herder who leaves ninety-nine sheep in a safe place and travels with great effort to rescue the one lost sheep. Then there is a story of a woman who loses a coin and goes on a search till she finds it. This is followed by the lost son or you may know this story as the 'prodigal son' story, where a son takes his inheritance, throws and blows it away living a wild life, ends up destitute and desperate, humbles himself and returns home into his father's arms. All three are powerful, yet the one that has become my life's story is the shortest of the three. These are the three short verses, and hopefully I can explain why:

Luke 15:8-10 NIV[50]

"Or suppose a woman has ten silver coins and loses one. Doesn't she light a lamp, sweep the house and search carefully until she finds it? 9 And when she finds it, she calls her friends and neighbors together and says, 'Rejoice with me; I have found my lost coin.' 10 In the same way, I tell you, there is rejoicing in the presence of the angels of God over one sinner who repents."

The woman is the God figure in this story and the coins are humanity. I just want to point out that this is not how the developed world thinks. If we lose some money, chances are we'll not throw away good money after bad. We know we can invest the remaining nine coins, earn interest, and in time replace the lost one without going to all the effort of searching for it. There are cultural considerations to this story that suggest possibly the coins were worn around her head and represented a dowry for her future husband. To the woman every coin was valuable. This is the same principle with the sheep story. Why, when there are still ninety-nine perfectly good, healthy, happy sheep, would you leave them to go after one lost, rebellious, stupid, wandering sheep? If you look after the other sheep, the sheep will get together and have more sheep and the lost one will be replaced.

Here is what I have learnt. This is never how God works. Jesus was a Rabbi and therefore used communications techniques used by Rabbis to get His message across. Exaggeration is one of those tech-

---

50 Holy Bible, *New International Version*, 1973, 1978, 1984, International Bible Society. Zonderzan Publishing House Luke 15:8-10

niques. Would the shepherd actually carry the sheep home and throw a party to celebrate? Probably not, but they all knew they would go after it because of its value. It's the same with the coin illustration. Jesus was teaching those listening, that despite anyone's current circumstances, they are of great intrinsic value. Jesus was actually leading a revolution to change mindsets in a culture self-dominated, rife with segregation, discrimination, violence and racial prejudice. Why? Because people are never disposable, no one is just a number; people are the most valuable thing on planet earth. Not because of their great skills and abilities. Not because of their efforts and achievements. They are valued simply because they are.

Consider this with me - if I was holding a one-dollar coin in my hand and I asked you, "What is it worth?" the answer would be one dollar. It's not a trick question! If I were to take that same coin and throw it out into the garden, what would it be worth? One dollar. If I took that same coin and let it sit under the stairs in the dust and grime for so long that it was forgotten about and it became filthy dirty, how much would that coin be worth? That's right - still one dollar. Here's where it's easy for us to get it wrong. However, God reveals His perspective here. The value of a coin was not dependent upon its location or condition. We tend to think that our value depends on our location, condition and circumstances, don't we? Therefore the value of a CEO of a large multinational corporation is so much higher than the value of a hotel employee who makes beds all day and has a limited income and education. Wrong! That's not how God thinks at all. The drunk on the street corner may or may not be there through poor decisions and circumstances, but his value as a human is still the same as the high-flying CEO. I'm not picking on any CEO. I'm simply making a point that our western perspective on value is vastly different to God's perspective. I'm all for high achievements and I've held important positions within organisations. These are great things, just like Gold medals.

Imagine with me for a moment that everyone reading these pages comes to a fundamental revelation, that if everything was stripped away, all the possessions, positions, perks and privileges, every single one of us would be able to confidently stand, knowing we are valued simply because we are.

Where does the value of the coins come from? The value of the coins is set when they were created and stamped with a seal. In Australia the value is marked by the Queen's head. It may be a King for you, or president or governmental seal etc. These vary from country to country however in God's economy all are of the same value, all have been marked, all have been created and are stamped with the Maker's mark and value. When we truly get this, I mean let it really get us - it changes everything. To know that my value is not based on my circumstances, abilities, achievements, location of birth, family heritage, and mistakes I've made. Nor abuses I've suffered, or my race, colour or creed. We are all of great value, from the Eskimo in the Arctic to the banker in Baltimore, from the unfortunate untouchables in the slums of Mumbai, to the lofty and unreachable of high caste Indian. From the outback bush blokes in Australia, to the uptown girls of New York, every one is important and every one of great intrinsic value, simply because they are.

In his book 'Too Small to Ignore' Dr. Wess Stafford, the former CEO of Compassion International, speaks of poverty when saying 'Poverty is an inside-out thing. It does its worst on the inside destroying the soul in teaching precious people that they don't matter.'[51] (I'm paraphrasing). I personally come across so many people of all ages, living every day in countries so free and full of many good things, yet

---

51 Stafford, Dr. Wess. *To Small To Ignore: Why the Least of These Matters Most.* Special Edition WaterBrook Press, Colorado Springs, Colorado

they are in poverty of their soul. They truly believe in their heart of hearts that they don't matter. Change this understanding and you change lives. This core belief changes everything.

When it comes to personal value, if our neural circuitry has been established in a way that defines us as of small value then it's time to begin a new pathway. Do this for the next 30 days; every day remind yourself of those three little verses about the coin. Every day simply read and re-read them, over and over again. When those old thinking patterns tell you what you've thought about yourself for years, capture the thought, reject it and replace it. Remember, we only conquer by replacing.

As we discuss the power of habits to rule our lives, you'll see how changing our habits of thinking constructs and re-enforces new pathways. When walked down often enough, they strengthen and transform our lives. It's so cool; I cannot wait to get there.

Recently while speaking in a gathering of people, I read a passage of scripture and a young lady along the front row began to cry. This was not just crying. She sobbed and her tears, you could tell, were the bitterest tears of all. The meeting was drawing to a close and while others were affected and comforted, this young lady was inconsolable. This precious amazing person had done some things she was so ashamed of that she considered herself as worthless. She actually viewed herself as a murderer due to the choices she'd made over her unborn children. Thankfully that day these verses below started a change for her life. She was able to see herself not in the darkness of her mistakes but in the light of a God who sees all, forgives all, and is all loving.

Another scripture states:

"Can a mother forget the infant at her breast,
walk away from the baby she bore?

> But even if mothers forget,
> I'd never forget you—never.
> Look, I've written your names on the backs of my hands."
> Isa 49:15-16 (Msg)[52]

This passage uses some fascinating visual imagery. Even looking at the last line, "Look, I've written your names on the back of my hands," we can get a visual image in our minds. We can think of how someone writes something on their hand with a pen so they don't forget. With a little examination of the original language we see that the meaning literally goes much deeper. Pen washes off, yet the true meaning is that God has etched or engraved our names into his hands. That's our value to Him. That doesn't come off! I think that's His point. He can never forget us and He's gone through pain to make it that way.

---

52 Eugene H. Peterson The Message: The Bible in Contemporary Language. NavPress Colorado Springs, Colorado 80935 p.979-980

WIDE

Arms open wide

Consider this; if I were to be standing before you with both my arms stretched out in opposite directions, and in my left hand I placed everything attributed to God within the world today, we'd have buildings, books, banners, properties, pulpits, pews, sanctuaries, stationary, statues, stages, sound systems, stained glass windows, lighting, lecterns, liturgy, and so forth. Think of this. Around the world billions upon billions of dollars' worth of stuff all placed in one hand, all dedicated to God and His church, all used for his purpose and for the common good of mankind. There is nothing wrong with these things, but let me explain the heart and nature of God. There sits everything, everything that we tend to think God likes or wants, yet, alone in my other hand is you. Just you, no masks, there you are. All your past, the good, the bad, the broken, battered, bruised, messed up, marginalised, medicated, hassles, hang-ups and hurts. The lot!

Please never forget this as long as you live, because this is the heart of God. Two arms stretch out and everything is in the balance. Which do you think God would choose? The choice is all the amassed items around this globe attributed to Him, all the billions upon billions of dollars' worth of stuff, all those beautiful blue stone buildings and

WIDE

spectacular spires, stunning sanctuaries, or one solitary person? This I know. God will choose you every time! Every—single—time, without fail or hesitation! Why? Because to God the true treasure of heaven and earth is you. Not perfect, just you! All the other stuff may

> *Buildings were built by men,*
> *yet a man's soul was built by God.*

be fine, yet a human life is reserved for eternity. Buildings were built by men, yet a man's soul was built by God. The bible tells us that eternity is set in the hearts of mankind.[53] There my friend is some

---

53 Holy Bible, *New International Version*, 1973, 1978, 1984, International Bible Society. Zonderzan Publishing House Ecclesiastes 3:11

seriously good news!

So once this understanding becomes settled within our lives, how does it change things? Well, think about this; a random thought invades your day. This thought tells you that, according to your past, you are fooling yourself to think that God, or anyone else for that matter, could ever really love you. However, once you know your value, having come to terms with the fact that your value to God is beyond anything past, present or future, then and only then, it becomes easier to identify and isolate that thought, bring it into captivity, identify it as destructive, and deal with it accordingly. That makes sense, doesn't it?

WILL

Now it's an act of will

Much like engaging the gears of a motor vehicle begins movement, we must engage the will. Moving forward towards wellness is vital. You know it, now do it. To add a little framework around the process, let me share a little secret I learned from a leader many years ago. He said to me, "When you trip, get up so quick nobody notices." I would like to pass on the same advice. There will be times within the pursuit of wellness when you will not get it right, when the thoughts will sneak through, days when you will simply take the old path to the river. The tendency when that happens, will be to throw your hands in the air and think you've messed it up and you'll never be able to achieve the sound mind you so desire. This is of course not true! Remember, the mind resists change. If you're over twenty-five years of age, your brain has become fully developed. You have already established and strongly reinforced neural networks in place. Your 'wet concrete' has hardened and it will take time and a lot of effort to break through the surface.

I remember working with a plumber for a while, years ago. In one of our jobs we had to break apart a section of concrete to lay a pipe. To achieve the desired result I had to dig deep, literally. The hot sun hammering from above as I jackhammered the concrete beneath my feet. Piece by backbreaking piece, the concrete came apart, and although the work was difficult and perspiration drenched my body, the job was completed. Sometimes smashing up the old stuff is difficult, but it's worth the sweat.

Your mind will actively attempt to repel your rebellion against your set pathways. Yet remember also that although it may be hard at times and victory may seem a great distance away, even an impossible hope, the truth is, it is possible and victory is won, one day at a time. Therefore, get up and fight another day. The plain cold truth is that you and I will not win every battle. That's not the point. The goal is to win the war! Persistent advancement and replacement will attain the victory. In the words of a great leader who himself battled with his mind, Sir Winston Churchill at the depths of England's struggle against the seemingly overwhelming might of Nazi Germany during WWII said, "We shall fight on the beaches, we shall fight

> *Victory is won, one day at a time.*

on the landing grounds, we shall fight in the fields and in the street, we shall fight in the hills; we shall never surrender"[54]... In another great speech, Churchill summoned all his eloquence as he addressed the House of Commons on the 13th of May 1940. Although he spoke of the threat of Nazis Germany, his answer should be our answer related to our invading thoughts. It is indeed the answer within this book. It is my prayer that this cry will ring in each heart

---

54 Churchill, Winston S. The International Churchill Society. Speech to the house of Commons, May 4th, 1940 http://www.winstonchurchill.org/resources/speeches/1940-the-finest-hour/blood-toil-tears-and-sweat (accessed March 7th 2017)

every day from this time forth. I quote: "You ask, what is our aim? I can answer in one word: It is victory, victory at all costs, victory in spite of all terror, victory, however long and hard the road may be; for without victory, there is no survival."[55]

May I say, you ask, what is our aim? What is the aim of this book? Victory! Victory one day at a time. Victory one thought at a time. Victory, one captive at a time, one conscious frontal lobe decision at a time and victory, one layered memory in our Hippocampus at a time. Victory, one choice at a time, victory one step on the new path to the river, for over time this will produce a renewed mind and together we shall have our victory between our ears. "Victory in spite of all terror, victory, however long and hard the road may be; for without victory, there is no survival," Churchill proclaimed.[56] Today there is a revolution to begin! A battle to be waged! Join me on the barricades, wave the flags, stand against the tyranny of destructive thoughts and fight and never give up.

---

55 Churchill, Winston S. The International Churchill Society. Speech to the house of Commons, May 13th, 1940 http://www.winstonchurchill.org/resources/speeches/1940-the-finest-hour/blood-toil-tears-and-sweat (accessed March 7th 2017)

56 Churchill, Winston S. The International Churchill Society. Speech to the house of Commons, May 13th, 1940 http://www.winstonchurchill.org/resources/speeches/1940-the-finest-hour/blood-toil-tears-and-sweat (accessed March 7th 2017)

NOW

John Maxwell writes, "It may sound trite, but today is the only time we have. It's too late for yesterday. And you can't depend on tomorrow. That's why today matters."[57] I believe there is incredible power in today. Although everything in and around our lives has led us to right now, it's everything right now that will lead us to our tomorrows. I know that doesn't sound that profound, however, from my experience humans are generally very poor at enjoying today. We tend to be lost in our yesterdays or so engrossed in our planning tomorrow, that we miss the magic of the moment. Living in the power of today does not mean that we act recklessly today and thus destroy our future. It's quite the opposite actually. Living in the power of today means to make choices now, which will open our futures'. The first step in this process is to own our today. In fact, it's owning our today that will open our tomorrow.

Paralysis

Many precious people are so paralysed by their past or living in a fantasy of their future, that they miss the miracle of the moment.

We talked earlier about controlling our thought life. Never is this

---

[57] Maxwell, John C. *Today Matters 12 Daily practices to guarantee tomorrow's success*. Centre Street, Hachette Book Group. New York, NY 10017. P. 10

more important than when it comes to our past. This is especially important if our past has been filled with significant challenges. Life is actually a lot like modern flying. There's parking, waiting, queuing, waiting, checking in, waiting, boarding, traveling from place to place with probably more queuing and waiting. This seemingly mundane process is punctuated by moments of delight and at times fear. The analogy is not perfect but I hope you get the picture. On flights we take baggage. Imagine if we always took the same old baggage and only added more to it each flight. I know that sound ridiculous. Yet how many people never let go of their past baggage and they take it on every flight. The challenge is that it doesn't take long before the aircraft is so heavy it cannot take off, not to mention the cost of all that excess baggage. There's a huge cost to carrying all that excess baggage and your plane will end up grounded or life will 'crash and burn' around you. The truth is that what we carry with us will either help or hinder our lives. It will either lighten us, enabling us to fly further, higher and faster, or weigh us down. How silly would an aircraft look, constantly taxiing, yet so weighed down it's never able to fly?

We all have regrets. Trying and failing is part of life, isn't it? The problem arises in continuing to carry everything from our past with us. We will carry some of our past, as all our past experiences add up to who we are today. Mistakes are a normal part of life, as someone once said, "He who never made a mistake, never made anything."[58] Are not even the basics of life a process of learning from mistakes?

I could take you to the place where one of my daughters took her first steps. She had been moving around on the furniture for a while and now those first tentative steps were taken. As a parent, pure joy

---

58 Quote Investigator. Exploring the origins of Quotations. The Person Who Never Makes a Mistake Will Never Make Anything. http://quoteinvestigator.com/2014/12/16/no-mistakes/ (accessed March 7th 2017)

is in these moments. We encourage them to walk. Yet walking is actually a process of stopping a fall. What if a child after taking a few feeble learning steps, falls and refuses to try again. We would think of them as foolish, wouldn't we? "Come on"; "You can do it"; "Well done"; "Up you get" are things we say while standing them up ready to launch again.

Just as you don't know all I've been through to get here, I don't know your story. We each have a story, it is unique, beautiful, and has its own set of challenges to be overcome. Each story has good and bad, light and darkness. Someone once noted that it's actually the dark colours that give a work of art its definition. Yet the thing that everyone who arrives at life's great destinations has in common is the tenacity to keep trying. Now if you've just thought something like, "I would but…" then it's time to tell the 'buts' to 'but out'.

RERUNS

There are some visual images you cannot un-see. There are situations and traumas you cannot undo. There are mental, emotional and physical stimuli that affect us so deeply that we replay then many times over in our minds. We see them again and again in our mind's eye. We feel them over again through our emotions. Every rerun connects emotionally and to some degree we relive the initial experience over again. This next story illustrates what I mean.

It was nearing the Sunday before Christmas. I was looking forward to enjoying my home church. I was not down to speak, so catching up with great friends after a busy schedule was high on my agenda. Little did I know that sickness had ravaged the minister's household and I would end up speaking that Sunday, and that it would be an essential breakthrough day for so many. Christmas is a great celebration and I enjoy it immensely, yet for many, Christmas is an entirely different story. Australian Christmases are generally warm, filled with long days and plenty of sunshine. Within our culture people gather with family and much time is spent outdoors, playing, eating, drinking and eating more and in some cases drinking far too much. As nice as all those festivities sounds, for some it's a traumatic experience. Family members arrive who you've not seen for at least a year. They eat your food, mess up your house and in some cases, you don't even really like them. I'm just being real here. Now, before you tell me that you read my bio and I'm a minister and therefore should like everyone – really?? There are some people I never want to see at Christmas, or anytime for that matter. I'll choose to love them, but like them, well..?.

In the auditorium that day was a young lady I had known for many years. She is a practical thinker, even in temper, a little shy and genuinely one of the nicest people you could meet. Yet this morning I noticed something I'd never seen in her before. She was deeply unsettled. For a while now she had known a particular relative was coming for Christmas and was to stay in her home for a few days. She was in a spiral of escalating anxiety. The reason for this was a trauma suffered by her many years ago involving this relative. Over recent months she'd been playing the scene over and over again in her mind. Her thoughts had been dominated by it and every day signaled another step toward the impending, unavoidable tension of the encounter.

For many, the arrival or even the thought of some people arriving

> ***We cannot take hold of our future when our past has hold of us.***

brings up memories and hurts from their past. Launching into this section on forgiveness, I want to encourage you that neurologically, this is not just important, but it's vital to winning between the ears. Earlier I talked about an eagle in a cage and that I might rattle some cages in order to see people set free. This part might rattle your cage. Sorry if it does, but just keep going. I've found there's nothing that cages people and their potential more than the past. That is why each one of us must, if we're to reach our potential, learn to forgive and move forward.

We cannot take hold of our future when our past has hold of us.

DESTRUCTIVE MEMORY LOOPS

There are people in my life that just the mention of their name will fire my brains amygdala. The amygdala is our fight or flight mechanism. It connects directly to our hippocampus where the bulk of our layered memories are stored. Therefore I hear the name, my amygdala fires, my memories shoot toward my decision making centre in the frontal lobe, a heap of other chemicals start flooding my body and I choose fight or flight. This process is largely subconscious and it all happens in a fraction of a millisecond. The challenge is that as the memories surface, if they contain trauma, in a sense we relive the pain, hurt and anger of that trauma. You know yourself how easy it is to get lost in these thoughts, isn't it? Therefore in the example of someone who sparks negative layered memories coming for Christmas dinner, I'm already in a heightened state of awareness; fight or flight mode is activated and my body is pumping adrenaline. This process produces heightened tension, anxiety and responsiveness. These brain mechanisms are stunningly efficient and are designed to save our lives. It's the amygdala that would fire at the sound or hint that a sabre-tooth tiger is nearby. The layered memories tell me it will not end well if it eats me and therefore this cave man runs for cover or prepares to fight.

These brain responses are healthy for survival, yet one of the dangers of our current society is that people are living in the state of constant tension and their amygdala is firing continually. This is why anxiety is at record levels and people are collapsing mentally at rates never before seen in humanity. This mechanism within our brains is designed for speed, efficiency and effective action. It's also designed to be something switched on and off rather then left on for extended periods. On that Sunday before Christmas, I spoke on forgiveness and later chatted with my friend who was spiraling deeper into anxiety. This became the starting point to freedom. It became the catalyst for a process of identifying the trauma, knowing the physical processes of the mind and the beginning of walking a path toward forgiveness and wholeness. The destructive memory loops firing her amygdala as she relived in part the childhood trauma, were resulting in anxiety, yet thankfully it was the case of right message for the right day and it helped her through what was still a difficult time.

FOCAL-ISM

Focalism or 'Anchoring' is a cognitive bias. [59] It's when we take one piece of information and rely heavily on this perception when making future decisions. Known as the 'anchoring effect', Science Daily states this is a 'common human tendency.'[60] The ability for the brain to focalise is great in the positive, yet destructive in the negative.

For instance, I could take you to the exact location I became a victim of focalism. There I was, 23 years old, harmlessly sitting at a café looking over the main business district in Coffs Harbour. While enjoying a coffee with a friend, unexpectedly, it happened! All of a sudden this bank employee walked past, dressed in her stylish uniform with a straight skirt, long legs, blazer and flowing spiral-permed hair. At that moment as I gazed upon a vision of splendour strolling by, I fell hopelessly victim to focalism. So focused was I that there could have been cars crashing, bombs exploding, singers singing or someone doing cartwheels down the main street, yet all I could see was her. Granted, a willing victim of focalism, I married her a year later and I'm happy to say, I'm still a major victim of focalism when it comes to

---

59 Program on Negotiation. Harvard Law School. Anchoring Effect. http://www.pon.harvard.edu/tag/anchoring-effect/ (accessed March 7th 2017)

60 Science Daily. Anchoring bias in decision-making. https://www.sciencedaily.com/terms/anchoring.htm (accessed March 7th 2017)

Robyn. I know, it's a corny example but I hope you get the picture that sometimes focalism is a good thing. It's good, as the memory loops developed regarding Robyn are a positive distraction. Where focalism becomes destructive is when my memory loops are negative and contain hurt or trauma. To explain this better I want to introduce you to a focalism sufferer. This guy became so focused on one thing that he missed something incredible. We do this when we let our regrets, failures and unforgiveness focus our thought patterns. I want to be sensitive here. Please know that I'm not in any way saying that forgiveness is an easy thing, nor for that matter, a quick thing either. I have had people in my life that it's taken years to truly forgive them, including forgiving myself. Yet it's powerful when we do, and releases us for our future. Martin Luther King Jr. once stated;

"Forgiveness is not an occasional act: it's a permanent attitude."[61]

---

61 King, Martin Luther Jr. *Dream. The words and inspiration on Martin Luther King Jr.* Hachette Australia Level 17, 207 Kent St Sydney NSW 2000Australia p. 29

TARDIS

To get to this focalism sufferer, I need to transport you back about 2000 years. I like Sci-fi and I'm a bit of a Dr. Who fan so I can imagine flying back to the ancient Near East in the first century in a TARDIS. If it helps, just imagine your personal time machine transporting you. This is important, because if we view this story through 21st century eyes we miss so much. Imagine with me you're there 2000 years ago, possibly wearing a turban, sandals, robe and leather strap as a belt. Ladies, you can imagine you're covered head to toe. I know, not particularly fetching but that's the way it was. You're sitting listening to an ancient teacher known as a Rabbi. He begins to tell a story to explain to everyone listening how they should approach forgiveness. The common thinking of the time, and promoted by several teachers of the day, was that you would choose to forgive others three times if they wronged you. One of this Rabbi's main students thought he'd figured it all out and suggested that three was incorrect and seven was the right number. Then the Rabbi uses this story to expand their minds and hopefully their hearts when it comes to forgiving others.

This Rabbi is about to use an interesting and common (for the time) communication technique called a 'hyperbole'. Ancient teachers of the day would use this form of purposeful exaggeration to express their meaning. They would take their point and exaggerate it to the point of almost ridiculous and humorous lengths, in order that their listeners would engage in their message and grasp the key concept. 'Hyperbole' comes from the ancient Greek language meaning 'excess, exaggeration, throwing beyond or long throw.'[62] According to the English dictionary a 'hyperbole' is an 'obvious and intentional exaggeration.'[63] It is not meant to be taken literally. We use these all the time. Have you ever said, "I'm so hungry I could eat a horse!" Well you're probably not that hungry, but you want to communicate to someone that you're after something to eat. In my case, Robyn is always the last one to leave most places we attend. She rates high for interpersonal interaction and a conversation is always to her of greater priority than a time schedule. I, on the other hand, although liking a good conversation, also know when I want to leave and therefore invariably desire to leave earlier then Robyn. So I find myself saying things like, "I waited for Robyn, for...ever!" Well, did I actually wait forever? Well, no. I exaggerated to prove or express a point. Some ladies I've heard say, "These heels are killing me!" Well they're actually not. Yes, they may be doing irreparable damage to your spinal cord, but they're not killing you. These are all purposeful exaggerations not to be taken literally, but to express a point.

To the suggested seven times to forgive, the Rabbi says, "Not seven, but seventy times seven."[64] This is a massive differential. From three to seven is over double, but now 490 times? That's ridiculous. The teacher then launches into an illustrative story that for the 1st

---

62 Dictionary.com Hyperbole. http://www.dictionary.com/browse/hyperbole (accessed March 7th 2017)

63 Dictionary.com Hyperbole. http://www.dictionary.com/browse/hyperbole (accessed March 7th 2017)

64 Holy Bible, *New International Version*, 1973, 1978, 1984, International Bible Society. Zonderzan Publishing House Matthew 18:22

century listener is so ridiculous that this 'long throw' is beyond belief. Yet this is exactly the Rabbi's plan, to use exaggeration, taking the topic to ridiculous extremes, to prove a point.

You might have gathered it's a biblical story because your TARDIS has landed you in the 1st century. If you have a bit of bible knowledge I want you to pretend you're hearing about this for the first time. I want you to see yourself there and view this through 1st century eyes. If you've had nothing to do with the bible, then first time should be easy.

The story progresses with a king settling accounts with his servants. Two thousand years ago the world ran on servants and while this story is not condoning slavery it uses current reality to express a point. Two servants owed the king money. So as the king began to settle accounts, "a man who owed him ten thousand talents was brought to him."[65] Why 10,000? Here is where it's very important that we take a 1st century view. Today we think 10,000. That's big, but my car may have cost me more and my house certainly did. Yet then, this was a purposeful exaggeration or long throw that was beyond reality or comprehension. Where today our largest number is called a Googolplexian, at that time 10,000 was the largest number in existence and entire nations didn't have that sort of money. Equating to approximately $6 billion in our money, this was so far out there, so utterly ludicrous, that each one sitting in the room would have collectively thought, "No way man, impossible." That's of course the point, this guy's debt was impossible to repay. He says he will repay everything but every listener knows how preposterous that thought is. So the master had pity on him and forgave his debt - all of it, every last bit.

---

65 Holy Bible, *New International Version*, 1973, 1978, 1984, International Bible Society. Zonderzan Publishing House Matthew 18:24

Not only is this a great picture of rescue and forgiveness for all our wrong doings, we can see that this first servant could have walked away as free as a bird. Just imagine how free he was at that moment. All the weight of such a huge debt was gone. No repayments needed. He should have gone from that place singing and dancing in all the freedom of a man released. He was for that brief moment as free as a bird. From that moment there was nothing holding him back except himself. How would you feel at this point? Elated I'd imagine. But look at what happens next. This man, the $6 billion in debt man, now a moment later a debt free man, the guy who should have been doing cartwheels down the main street with gratitude for all the forgiveness he had received, now steps outside the room. I would have hugged everything in sight and danced all the way home. Yet this man spotted another servant. Here the master communicator now brings his long throw message on forgiveness and drops it back in our laps to drive the point home. You hear him say, "But when the servant went out, he found one of his fellow servant who owed him a hundred denarii. He grabbed him and began to choke him."[66] This is the part where everything inside me doesn't like this guy. He does get his just desserts later on, but let's see something here. So you're in the crowd, and in the crowd listening this day would have been some who had a debt of around 100 denarii. This was a common debt and equated to around four months wages. Let me ask you a question. At this point, was the guy who had just been forgiven of such a massive debt, free? Well, no. Here we find him pinning someone else to the wall, choking them. If you're gripping someone else by the neck, are you free? No. This guy who had just been released, had all possibilities open to him and could walk away with his fu-

---

66 Holy Bible, *New International Version*, 1973, 1978, 1984, International Bible Society. Zonderzan Publishing House Matthew 18:28

ture open to amazing possibilities. He becomes a victim of negative focalism, to the point where for the sake of a small debt, traps himself. Imagine now if this man realised the destructive nature of his focalism and chose to stop choking the other guy. He could have got on with his life in the joy of his huge debt being gone. Yet if we follow the story through we see that he lost all his freedom because he trapped himself in unforgiveness.

Here's the point, unforgiveness traps the one holding on to it. He was forgiven, yet he refused to forgive. Right, now you might be thinking, "I see that, but it's hard to forgive." Yes it is. Tyler Perry says, "It's not an easy journey, to get to a place where you forgive people. But it is such a powerful place, because it frees you."[67] Now I've heard this story delivered with the thought that what we have to forgive is nothing in

> *"It's not an easy journey, to get to a place where you forgive people. But it is such a powerful place, because it frees you."*

comparison to what we've been forgiven of. I think there's more to it then that. If the teacher wanted to say that what we must forgive is nothing, why did he put a value on it? He could have said, "One denarii or less, but he didn't. Yes, in comparison to our forgiveness, what we need to forgive may be small, however it's never nothing. Jesus places a value on all we've been through in our lives. He's saying that the things we've suffered and the debts we're owed are real and of value, yet despite this, choosing to forgive will set us free. The longer we hold on, choking the debtor, the longer we are trapped and cannot live in all the freedom and wonder of our personal debt being forgiven.

---

67 Perry, Tyler. Brainy Quote Forgiveness Quotes. http://www.brainyquote.com/quotes/quotes/t/tylerperry418193.html?src=t_forgiveness (accessed March 7th 2017)

"The Weak can never forgive. Forgiveness is the attitude of the strong." Mahatma Gandhi[68]

In my life, I had someone who abused their privileged position in my life, used intimidation and became an abuser of many people. Although this was never physical, it was certainly psychological and verbal. I suffered under this regime of ill treatment for over ten years. It happened, and I must confess that forgiving that person has not been an easy or short journey. For years, every time his name came up, all those layered memories with raw and hurtful emotions attached would flood my mind, increasing tension and sending anxiety levels spiraling through the roof. There was nothing about this that was trivial and I had to go through the process of forgiving not only that person but myself, for putting up with it for so long. Every time these thoughts would flood my mind I had to go against my feelings and against any idea of justice. It was wrong behavior, nothing could justify it, and sadly no apologies would ever be forthcoming. Yet a choice to forgive over and over again was the only way to free myself from the tyranny of these injustices. I had to let go, for not only was I locked into the choking but also while ever I kept hold, I figuratively stayed in the presence of that person. They were always there just

> "The Weak can never forgive.
> Forgiveness is the attitude of the strong."
> Mahatma Gandhi

below the surface. Time and time again, despite all emotion attached, I had to choose to forgive. It took a long time yet I remember when I realised I had crossed the line into forgiveness. It happened

---

68 Gandhi, Mahatma. Brainy Quote Forgiveness Quotes. https://www.brainyquote.com/quotes/quotes/m/mahatmagan121411.html?src=t_forgiveness (accessed March 7th 2017)

that one day this person's name was mentioned, and instead of hurt, anger, regret and sadness, I was calm and felt pity and was able to genuinely pray for that person. My amygdala didn't fire and peace resulted, in fact I was able to get on with my life, enjoying all I'd been forgiven of. Make no mistake, I'm thrilled that person has no voice in my life or my family and I'm happy that way. Forgiving certainly doesn't mean forgetting, nor does it mean allowing negative influences to regain their position on our lives. If what I've been discussing is important to you, choose to let go. At least choose to begin the forgiveness process. Start a new neural pathway today. Take a new path to the river. It may be tough but you can do it. Over the existing layered memories, begin laying new ones filled with the choice to forgive.

> *"We must develop and maintain the capacity to forgive. He who is devoid of the power to forgive is devoid of the power to love."*

Love is the desired result of this story. That the one forgiven of so much would choose, because of what they've received, to love and forgive the other person. Martin Luther King Jr. connected the relationship between love and forgiveness well: "We must develop and maintain the capacity to forgive. He who is devoid of the power to forgive is devoid of the power to love."[69]

---

[69] King Martin Luther Jr. Brainy Quote Forgiveness Quotes. http://www.brainyquote.com/quotes/quotes/m/martinluth143179.html?src=t_forgiveness (accessed March 7th 2017)

SO FAR SO GOOD

Winning between the ears begins with our thought life.

Have you decided to forge a new path to the river?

Are you taking those first tentative steps into the unknown?

Machete in hand, you've commenced the process, determined to grow better neural pathways and thus produce a transformed mind. It's scary, yes, but worth every step. Hacking at the old layered memories, you're starting to slowly make progress. Slow is okay, because this is a process and you're metamorphosing as we speak. Besides, we're building a life here and it's worth the extra effort.

Perhaps you've known that you are locked in a cage of destructive thinking but the eagle inside you is determined to fly again. Oh, and you will. You'll fly higher, see further and be more majestic than ever before.

Together we've seen how biblical neuroscience works and how there's a new language to learn.

You may not have purchased those little boxes to wear on your head to work, school or on holidays, but by now the concept should be clear.

As you're slashing the forest before you, your mind may be telling you, "It's not worth it the old way is easier." But you know how to capture those thoughts now, and treat them accordingly.

You're like Napoleon, replacing conquered thoughts with better thinking.

You're working out your true value:

Are you enough even without the Gold medals? Absolutely! You are valued far beyond the human mind's ability to perceive fully, just because you are.

So with the power of today in mind and equipped with the knowledge of how, what and most importantly why, we must develop new neural pathways. We look to the future.

Have you cleared the decks of the clutter of the past and unloaded the excess baggage keeping you grounded?

You've forgiven all and set yourself free from its power overcoming those destructive memory loops or at least begun the process.

You have taken Martin Luther's advice and are 'maintaining the capacity to forgive'[70] therefore you have the capacity to truly love. You're in a good place right now. It will take work. Defeating wrong thinking and creating new, better processes is never instant or easy. But you've made a start, well done! "A journey of a thousand miles begins with a single step."[71]

---

70 King Martin Luther Jr. Brainy Quote Forgiveness Quotes. http://www.brainyquote.com/quotes/quotes/m/martinluth143179.html?src=t_forgiveness (accessed March 7th 2017)

71 Tzu, Lao. Brainy Quotes.com Lao Tzu Quotes https://www.brainyquote.com/quotes/quotes/l/laotzu137141.html (Accessed February 28th 2017)

BREAKFAST

Habits change everything. In his 1981 hit 'Bad Habits', Billy Field sang;
"Well I'm off the rails,
My resistance fails
Temptations got a hold on me,
And I can't refuse, because I always lose.
Can't help myself, Bad Habits."[72]

Habits eat good intentions for breakfast
How true it is, that generally the established habit wins. We can have all the right intentions, make some quality decisions and have truck-

> *Habits eat good intentions for breakfast*

loads of determination and desire, but it will all account for nothing unless we understand the power of habits. Habits rule! It's as simple as that.

In fact, changing our thinking patterns to win between our ears

---

[72] Field, William Bruce(Billy)/Price, Thomas Shelton. Bad Habits Warner/Chappell Music, Inc.

and re-write our neural pathways thus forging that new and better path to the river only happens as we create new habits. We as human beings, function through habits. We discussed earlier how the brain is designed to be the most efficient mechanism on earth. In creating new neural pathways, repetition forms habits that make it possible for us to function at an optimum level. Without developed habits we would have to think about everything we do and we would simply not function well. John Ortberg states, "Mostly, our behavior is governed by habit. Most of the time, a change of behavior requires the acquisition of new habits."[73] This is true, as creating a new habit creates new neural networks which pattern the brain.

Ortberg also states, "Habits eat willpower for breakfast."[74] I would go as far as saying that life is not only dominated by our habits but determined by them also. "A habit is a relatively permanent pattern of behavior that allows you to navigate life. The capacity for habitual behavior is indispensable. When you first learn how to type or tie a shoe or drive a car, it's hard work. So many little steps to remember! But after you learn, it becomes habitual. That means it is quite literally 'in your body' (or 'muscle memory') at the level of your neural pathways."[75] The old classroom adage states: 'repetition is the master of learning.' This is true, as Dr. Raymond Andrews states, "There are two things required for renewal of the mind, focused thought and repetition."[76]

---

[73] Ortberg, John. Can Neuroscience Help Us Disciple Anyone? Brain science and renewal of your mind. http://www.christianitytoday.com/le/2014/summer/can-neuroscience-help-us-disciple-anyone.html?start=6

[74] Ortberg, John. Soul Keeping Caring for the most important part of you. Zondervan, Grand Rapids, MI 49546 P.70

[75] Ortberg, John. Can Neuroscience Help Us Disciple Anyone? Brain science and renewal of your mind. http://www.christianitytoday.com/le/2014/summer/can-neuroscience-help-us-disciple-anyone.html?start=6

[76] Andrews Dr. Raymond New Life Worldwide Ministries. Advanced Workshop.

We've touched on repetition already and how vital it is whether learning a new language or establishing an exercise regime. Dr. Caroline Leaf promotes her excellent 21-day detox where for seven minutes a day, for 21 days, you can eliminate toxic thinking. When I heard her speaking in Coffs Harbour recently she was promoting that people do the 21 days twice. I think that's wise. There is certainly a process in detoxing our thinking and there is also a process in establishing new non-toxic thought pathways. None of us will ever conquer old thinking patterns unless we replace them. Therefore, it's the conscious repetition and replacement of old thought patterns with new patterning that over time create habits. It's these habits that will determine our future more than anything else in our world.

'Neurologists call this process where the brain converts a sequence of actions into routine activity, 'chunking.'[77] 'The New York Times profiled the work on behavior and habits at M.I.T. A striking image and phenomena is what the researchers call 'chunking,' the process of converting sequences of familiar actions or behaviors into semi-autonomous actions.'[78] So what we need to do is personal, willpower driven, and life defining, 'chunking' on ourselves. All new skills require determined learning, dominated early by consistently directed willpower until the new skill becomes habitual. Imagine creating a habit where instead of thinking of ourselves falsely as inadequate or in any negative way, we embrace a new and more positive thought process and consciously focus repetitively for two months.

Coffs Harbour Cex Club. September 2014.

77 Ortberg, John. Can Neuroscience Help Us Disciple Anyone? Brain science and renewal of your mind. http://www.christianitytoday.com/le/2014/summer/can-neuroscience-help-us-disciple-anyone.html?start=6

78 Xraydelta Behavior Chunking – That's why change is tough https://xray-delta.com/2012/03/06/behavior-chunking-thats-why-change-is-tough/ (accessed March 7th 2017)

What a change there would be! We create a habit of conquering our old thinking patterns by replacing them with new thinking habits. Creating these new thinking habits will literally 'chunk' us into a better life. I did this and in the process of repetition new neural pathways developed and became stronger, to the point now that it has become the dominant pathway and has become a habit to think that way. Creating new habits changes everything. What if I were to take one piece of advice from a great scholar and make it my focal point till it became a habit? It would then become the lens through which I see the world. Then I would be a disciple of that scholar, wouldn't I? When our perceptions change, our worldview changes, for we never really see the world for what it is but rather from who we are. I've used the following scripture repeatedly to create a positive thought habit: "Finally, whatever is true, whatever is noble, whatever

> *Plan to create the habits that will define and re-define our neural pathways.*

is right, whatever is pure, whatever is lovely, whatever is admirable—if anything is excellent or praiseworthy—think about such things."[79] You can pick your own focal points, but this is not just a one-off decision. John Irving said, "Good habits are worth being fanatical about."[80] This is effective when adopted at any phase or age of life. Naturally the younger good habits are developed, the greater potential for positive life change. While Aristotle stated, "Good habits

---

79 Holy Bible, *New International Version*, 1973, 1978, 1984, International Bible Society. Zonderzan Publishing House Philippians 4:8

80 Irving, John Brainy Quotes.com John Irving Quotes http://www.brainyquote.com/quotes/quotes/j/johnirving378460.html (accessed March 7th 2017)

formed at youth make all the difference,"[81] continuing or beginning to form good habits when you get beyond youth, while they may not have the same compound effect as from a young age, will make a powerful difference in our lives.

Plan to create the habits that will define and re-define our neural pathways.

Forging the way takes conscious determination and repeatedly going that way takes willpower. We trained or 'chunked' ourselves into learning to drive a car, ride a bike and tie our shoelaces. We can therefore 'chunk' ourselves into thinking more positively about ourselves, about others and about the world around us.

Never let go of the 'Why' we needed a new path to the river in the first place. The 'Why' will drive the will till the habit becomes established. Aristotle said, "We are what we repeatedly do. Excellence then, is not an act, but a habit."

If Duhigg is correct when saying, "The Golden rule of habit change: You can't extinguish a bad habit, you can only change it,"[82] then alter it we must. If we consider the path to the river metaphor, we see that many elements are actually the same and therefore forging a new path to the river is an alteration of a journey for the better rather than a new journey altogether. For many it's more like steering then starting. In both cases the goal is the water from the river, the same cabin is exited and we still must navigate the forest. The

The effort comes in the conscious alteration until the unconscious habit is created.

---

[81] Aristotle Brainy Quotes.com Aristotle Quotes http://www.brainyquote.com/quotes/quotes/a/aristotle400385.html (accessed March 7th 2017)

[82] Duhigg, Charles. *The Power of Habit: Why we do what we do in life.* 2014 Random House Company, New York.

effort comes in the conscious alteration until the unconscious habit is created. It's the manual effort before the automatic kicks in. This is the bottom line of the matter. The transition between pathways is the creation of new habits. Walking the new and better way once is simply not enough. One decision, no matter how well intended, unless followed constantly, will not make permanent life change. The facts are simple, my neurological preferences or 'cravings' will dominate until new neurological 'cravings' out-crave the original ones.

MOTIVATE

Motivation and in fact motivational speakers are in some ways pretty useless. Please don't be offended if you're a motivational speaker. I've been referred to as one many times. I'd however rather the term 'inspirational speaker,' because true motivation is never something that can be drawn from another. It's internal, or as Covey puts it, an 'inside-out'[83] thing. There is nothing more 'inside-out' then creating new neurological pathways to metaphorical rivers. I can inspire you in this direction, but it's your personal motivation that will drive the results.

We've established that reading has always been challenging for me, and that I had discovered during secondary school I had always suffered from Dyslexia. I remember that remedial classes and after school tutoring were all used in desperation by my teachers and parents to help me read, but sadly in vain. One result was that I developed the art of surviving life without reading, producing habits of avoidance. Yet the time came in my life where I knew I would have to learn to read if I was ever going to achieve anything truly worthwhile. I know this must seem ridiculous to all who have never found reading difficult, yet at the

---

[83] Covey. Stephen R. *The 7 Habits of Highly Effective People: Powerful Lessons in Personal Change.* FranklinCovey Co, 2012

age of 23 with a reading level of 'Green Eggs and Ham'[84], I could not see myself aspiring to much in adult life. If I didn't take steps to overcome my learning difficulties, I would have been avoiding situations that could expose my Dyslexic wiring for the rest of my life. Therefore, I began a daily reading program. I would like to say that all of a sudden reading opened up to me, my Dyslexia dissipated and a university degree graduate, published author, I became. Although I claim some divine help in the process, the reality was that it all began as an act of will, founded in the self-motivation of 'The Why.' Thankfully from humble and slow beginnings this journey of discovery opened a world previously beyond my horizon. This journey to the unseen land of literature I now enjoy. Coming to that horizon has been filled with challenges and none more than the fight against biology. It began with a preemptive strike of pure, fearful, painful, stubborn determination that has now become a joyful path to the river I take every day.

The power of decision

Deciding to take a new path to the river cannot be just a preference. Preference says, "I'll go this way unless." It's the big 'if' in our choices. 'If' this works out I'll do that. 'If' all goes well we'll stay married. I'll keep at this job 'if'.... I'll continue to learn to read 'if' it's satisfying. A decision to create new pathways to the river cannot be an 'if' preference. Everything biologically and neurologically will push us habitually toward the old path. Let us be under no false illusions here, everything inside you will resist the change. The brain is designed to preference-established shortcuts and to use them as efficiently as possible. Although you desire change, your brain does not.

---

84 Dr. Seuss. *Green Eggs and Ham. Beginner Books: Random House*, 1960. New York, New York.

This is why a preemptive strike is vital. It's the decision before the decision. It's the conscious, practical, non-emotional choice made preemptively that will determine our success. When in a moment of stress our emotional reflexes engage chemical reactions, sound reason in the full light of day may not agree with these reactions. I have worked extensively with young people over many years. Let me tell you, that if a young lady waits till she's with a young man together in a car, parked somewhere late at night, to decide she'll put limits on how far they will proceed physically, it's generally too late. This is because the heightened emotional environment overcomes sensible sound-minded decisions. However, when the same young person,

> ***It's the conscious, practical, non-emotional choice made preemptively that will determine our success.***

male or female, decides pre-emptively that they will not proceed beyond a certain point, they have a far better chance of controlling the environment.

Creating a reading program for a Dyslexic early twenties young man had to be a preemptive decisive decision. Simply because absolutely nothing that had been patterned in my mind for twenty-three years even considered this as an option. Therefore the fight was on. The undergrowth was thick and every fibre of my being pushed me toward the known established paths and survival techniques. Right there, was the battle ground for the rest of my life. Right there was the beginning of winning between the ears.

One of my favourite things I get to do with my life now is to encourage the thousands of young people I come across who have various forms of learning difficulties. I encourage them that anything is truly possible, encouraging people who struggle with Dyslexia, that they're not stupid, dumb or weird; they're just wired differently. This relieves so much self-condemnation. I then inspire them that if they will take their natural wiring and create life-changing habits, they can achieve great things. I also get to travel and speak on some of the coolest material. None of this would have been possible if not for the creation of new habits.

Once I changed habits, habits changed everything else.

The battlefield began at age twenty-three. There in a one room converted garage under a house in Coffs Harbour, the battle lines were drawn. Twenty-three years of past established pathways, the formidable formative highly fortified frameworks established early in life stood armed and ready. The archers readied their bows with arrows of past pain, failed schooling, embarrassing moments, shame and insecurity. The battlements bristled with every spear of self-doubt, armed with catapults of schoolyard cruelty and soul piercing arrows of past defeats. There on the battlefield, facing this mighty mountain of memories and filled with fear, uncertain and overwhelmingly outnumbered, was one young man. How could he win? Surely this task was beyond one man. The odds were stacked

Once I changed habits, habits changed everything else.

overpoweringly against him. Truth be known, he didn't win all the time. Some days the enemy was simply too strong and the battle too hard. Yet day after day he came back to the line, day after day he opened the pages of a book and with ruler on page, started to slowly read. Three, four o'clock in the morning when all was quiet outside, the battle raged within. Little by little, day-by-day, like a steady drop of water dissolving a rock, despite all else, the habit of opening those pages was formed. Step by step the ruler traveled steadily lower on the page. Line by line the machete cut through the growth. Seemingly insignificant victories over time change battles. I love now the strange expressions on the faces of those who knew me early in my life when I tell them some scientific or theological book I'm currently reading. I don't find them easy to read and please don't think I'm some speed-reading guru, but I can read, which for me is miraculous. It's a joy beyond compare and a direct result of habits that have, and still do, change my life.

Now years later, my neurological cravings are re-patterned. Will I probably ever be a fluent and fast reader who reads publicly without even the smallest hesitation when approaching words of more than two syllables? I don't honestly know, and I don't honestly care!

I know this; habitual behaviours either hinder or help humanity. I just have to determine what habits my life will run by and be ruled by.

I am in possession of a re-wired, transformed, rejuvenated and renewed mind. Actually now, because of habit, my re-wired mind is in possession of me. Seth Godin states, "You don't win an Olympic gold medal with a few weeks of intensive training. There's no such thing as an overnight opera sensation. Great law firms or design companies don't spring up overnight…Every great company, every great brand, and every great career has been built in exactly the same way: bit by bit, step by step, little by little."[85] Let us 'inch

> **Habitual behaviours either hinder or help humanity.**

---

85 Godin, Seth *"Slowly I turned…Step by Step…Inch by inch…,"* Fast Company, May 2003, 72

by inch' transform our habits, and watch our habits transform us. Taking Maxwell's advice, "When it comes to success, you're better off hopping to it then hoping for it."[86] Let us ask the question; Where to from here?

I have a friend who loves reading books and regularly sends some my way. They're full of facts, figures, statistics, graphs, plans, strategies and envisaged outcomes. They are good books from some great experts in their fields. While I appreciate the gesture of sending me these books, give me a good biography any day. I love them. They're filled with human drama, challenges and overcoming. There are always those incredible moments in biographies, where the chips are down, trouble stands at every door and everything seems to be against the person. Then, from deep within the human spirit, comes the 'I'm going to walk again' moments. When all is lost with his face planted on the canvas, the fighter drags himself up for one more round and it's in that decision the rest of his life is determined. I

> *It is a great day in our lives when we realise that we are all writing our own biographies.*

hope during these pages, even while we've been deliberating on the neurological, biological and even theological, that you've connected with the very human nature of this story. It is a great day in our lives when we realise that we are all writing our own biographies. While we are all individuals and our stories vary greatly, I passionately believe that everyone can bring about personal transformation.

---

86 Maxwell, John C. *Today Matters 12 Daily practices to guarantee tomorrow's success.* Centre Street, Hachette Book Group. New York, NY 10017 p.5

TOTAL TRANSFORMATION

So where do you go from here? Well that depends on where you are. Large shopping malls mark their store locators with 'You are here' because knowing where you are is vital in order to go where you need to be. Therefore the obvious question is, 'Where are you?' That is a question only you can answer. Wherever you are, I hope these words have inspired you and these stories have given you hope, and not only hope, but a plan toward the future as well. I hope that you've seen the incredible connections between biblical truth and modern neuroscience. May you take these lessons and daily put them into operation. Although I cannot specify exactly what you need to do, as I don't know your story, I'm sure that while reading these pages you've probably come to an understanding and may already know what you must do next. There is a new and better path to the river for us all. It is my hope and prayer that this book has enhanced your life. May your mind be renewed, your hope lifted and your life transformed by the habits you create from now on. May you daily choose the new path to the river, until you, by habit, go that way automatically, for therein lies the secret of mind renewal and winning between the ears.

ABOUT THE AUTHOR

Gary Blackford is an author, speaker, minister, husband and father of four. 'Winning Between the Ears' follows his highly successful first book 'The Fog Lifter.'

Gary has pastored several churches, has been an international sales trainer to a Fortune 500 company, ran his own business and now helps people and churches transition forward. Theologically trained and equipped with a personal journey from total brokenness to complete wholeness, he uniquely connects with readers and listeners on a level few can.

Connect with him at **www.garyblackford.com**.

www.ingramcontent.com/pod-product-compliance
Lightning Source LLC
LaVergne TN
LVHW051502070426
835507LV00022B/2883